NOT ALL TWINS
ARE ALIKE

The author and her twin sister in Sapporo, Japan, in 1962.

NOT ALL TWINS ARE ALIKE

Psychological Profiles of Twinship

Barbara Schave Klein

Foreword by Marjorie Ford

PRAEGER

**Westport, Connecticut
London**

Library of Congress Cataloging-in-Publication Data

Klein, Barbara Schave.
    Not all twins are alike : psychological profiles of twinship / Barbara Schave Klein ;
        foreword by Marjorie Ford.
        p. cm.
    Includes bibliographical references and index.
    ISBN 0–275–97584–3 (alk. paper)
    1. Twins—Psychology. I. Title.
    BF723.T9 K57 2003
    155.44′4—dc21   2002029758

British Library Cataloguing in Publication Data is available.

Library of Congress Catalog Card Number: 2002029758
ISBN: 0–275–97584–3

First published in 2003

Praeger Publishers, 88 Post Road West, Westport, CT 06881
An imprint of Greenwood Publishing Group, Inc.
www.praeger.com

Printed in the United States of America

The paper used in this book complies with the
Permanent Paper Standard issued by the National
Information Standards Organization (Z39.48–1984).

10 9 8 7 6 5 4 3 2 1

To Elizabeth, Marjorie, Paul, and Richard.

Contents

Foreword

It was with great delight that I accepted the responsibility of writing the foreword to my identical twin sister's new book, *Not All Twins Are Alike*. Of course, it would seem like I'd be the natural candidate. But those of you who know about twin relationships may understand that twins don't always have "perfect" relationships. There have been many years when Barbara and I distanced ourselves from each other for a variety of reasons. We did not see ourselves as separate people and had unrealistic expectations of each other; we were competitive but did not like to admit that to ourselves or to each other. We were twins in a world where twins are only a tiny minority, and that made relationships with non-twins sometimes difficult and often confusing. Many people do not know how to act around twins. Unknowingly they may make observations and judgments about how they see a pair of twins; their remarks are often hurtful because comparing and contrasting twins is emotionally divisive for the twin pair. It is easy for twins, together and alone, to feel alienated from single-birthed people.

Scientific studies on twins have helped to illuminate the issue of nature versus nurture, whether our genes or our environment is more important in shaping an individual's personality. But not that much has been written for the general audience about twin identity. In fact, Barbara's first book on twins, which she developed from her Ph.D. dissertation, entitled *Identity and Intimacy in Twins* (1983), is one of a handful of books for a general audience that wants to know more about patterns of twinship and the struggles that twins go through to separate from each other and become strong and independent individuals, as well as loving twins. There are, of course, a number of coffee table books with striking photos of twins who look alike in their youth, in middle age, and into old age. These books are certainly remarkable to look at, but being a twin goes far beyond appearance. In reality, those coffee table books represent a profound irony at the heart of twinship. Because people tend to be so taken by the similarities in twins' appearances, they may forget to think more deeply and to try to understand what it might really feel like to have a double in the world. At birth each partner in the twinship begins to find a way to feel and to be an intensely unique individual.

How many of you have actually thought about what it might be like to have a living "double" who really looks like you, is clearly genetically similar to you, but who wants to be treated like an individual? To be truthful, one of the reasons some twins have problems in their relationship—and this was the case with us—is revealed in what one child said to her mother after the first day of a kindergarten class with Barbara and me: "Mom, I saw a girl with two heads." I don't think the child actually perceived us literally as being one person with two heads; it was her way of seeing us as "freaks." Many people do see twins as freaks, even if they don't acknowledge it, even to themselves. As children and young adults Barbara and I felt like freaks much of the time. We felt like we were a living comparison and contrast activity. Aunts and uncles, friends and strangers, mother and father—all of them had to differentiate us, and they didn't always think about being subtle. In reality, the opposite was true. Because we looked so much alike, they wanted to exaggerate our differences. That helped them get a grip on the unusual reality that we continued to represent.

I have spoken of some of the basic reasons why twins might have trouble relating to each other. But this is not my book, it is my twin's; she is the expert. I promise that you have a challenge and a treat ahead of you, learning, as you will, about all of the many complications that twins can have in their relationships. Barbara has entrusted me with the role of trying to capture representative moments from our childhood and youth that reflect "relationship truths" about us.

We were extremely close as children, and our mother dressed us alike, right down to the bracelets, necklaces, socks, and shoes that accompanied our dresses or play clothes. We slept in the same room, and we loved our Raggedy Ann wallpaper. We loved dolls of all kinds and played together to such an extent that we developed a private language of our own. To this day we can speak a private language that has rules. Still, our partners and children never seem to get the intonations of our language correct like we do.

Besides playing with our dolls, we loved to eat together. We loved to eat secretly together. Everyone in our family said we were too chubby and never offered us cookies or candy, but we were clever little chublets. We'd save our allowance and then walk a block and a half on some afternoons to Puris Market, where they had a bakery; there we'd purchase brownies. I especially remember eating our brownies, ever so slowly, until we got close to home. Till this day I doubt that anyone in our family knew about our afternoon adventures. Why would they? We were good eaters and always finished our dinner. I also remember having these competitions with Barbara to see who could eat our ice cream cone the most slowly. I can't remember who would usually win, but some members of our family found this ritual highly annoying. Even as children, we had an intuitive sense that we had power over others if we presented a united front. If I could go back to my childhood with Barbara, I would want to go on an afternoon stroll with our purses in hand to Puris Market to buy and eat brownies or have a slow-eating contest with ice cream cones. Those days are far in our past, but I still don't like to eat with other people.

Like many identical twins we were tricksters. We loved to trade our clothes in between classes so that our teachers, who could tell us apart only by memorizing our outfits, would inevitably call us the wrong name. Sometimes we took tests for each other. (In this case we did not trade clothes.) My French pronunciation was not impressive, so Barbara would sit in my seat and pass the test for me. Barbara, on the other hand, had difficulty with her Hebrew pronunciation and would argue with our uncle, who was the rabbi of our temple, that she was pronouncing all of the words correctly. I remember feeling humiliated because I didn't think she should argue with the rabbi and because I knew that she was wrong and because I knew that no one could tell us apart. In many variations and many situations, both Barbara and I felt humiliated when one of us acted in a way that the other wouldn't have, knowing full well that no one could tell us apart. In fact, Barbara finally did get confirmed. I stood in her place and read the Hebrew correctly.

Most of all as youngsters I think we focused our twin "demon" power on assembling a huge wardrobe because we loved clothes. By the time we were in junior high school, Mother had realized that she shouldn't be dressing us alike. Still, she never bought a new outfit for Barbara without buying one for me. That was one of Mother's cardinal rules. We took total advantage of the situation and assembled an amazing wardrobe. Dealing and swapping clothes became a favorite pastime. Even today we love to go shopping together, and we love trying to work out clothes swaps. I include a piece of a poem I wrote for Barbara when she turned 50, three minutes before me:

Jelly donuts
and custard long johns
and apple fritters
dripping with grease
sticky with sugar
BAD BAD BAD
like me
like you

the bad children
who will
never grow up
whose ageless spirit

only wants to play
making checkered cakes
raising our children
climbing mountains

listening to waterfalls
dancing

DKNY and Jeanne Marc,
Tahari and Christian and Ralph Lauren too
Aveda and La Prairie
they'll all bring gifts
to your
birthday party this special year
in The Garden of Red Roses

And when the Red Queen
has made her edict:
When she commands:
"Off with their heads!"
WE will remain
indifferent

intent only on our plan
we will walk
away

scheming about
the BIG
Upcoming
Trade . . .
the
deals
of all
time
ready for barter
still safely
in our bags.

Besides having fun tricking people and trading clothes, we loved to talk to and be with each other. We walked together to school and home from school from the day we started kindergarten until the day we graduated from high school. We did our homework together. We talked about our outfits and our boyfriends together. I was always giving her advice about her various boyfriends. She listened intently, but then did what she wanted. I took my role as adviser seriously, and Barbara had many, many boyfriends, so we never ran out of issues to discuss. We were never really alone until Barbara started dating, but still we knew a lot about each other's lives, even when we went off to college together.

I think, however, that the seeds of conflict in our relationship started during our college years. We both attended the University of California at Berkeley, where I was the Bohemian-intellectual twin who loved to hang out in the library or with my artist boyfriend, whom I married. Barbara was, at that time, the more emotional twin, in love with relationships, with the different men in her life. My way of separating from her was to become critical of what I saw in Barbara as maternal and materialistic. At the same time that I was separating from Barbara, I was separating from our mother. At that time I thought that I would never have children because too many parents, including ours, stayed married only "for the sake of the children." (Clearly I have changed, as my children are the dearest people in my life along with my husband, Barbara, and her two children.)

We were married within three weeks of each other. I went to live in Sweden on a University of California Study Abroad program with my new husband, and Barbara helped her new husband with his applications to medical school and got pregnant with her first child. This is when the times of struggle in our relationship began to intensify. We were embarking on different paths. Barbara married a man who was studying to be a doctor and had her children in her early 20s. After our year in Sweden my husband and I traveled all around Europe. Later we settled in London for two years, where I taught at a secondary school for girls and my husband attended London's Central School of Art and Design.

As I understand our relationship in retrospect, I was critical of Barbara. Now I feel ashamed for having been so superficial, for not trying to understand her life better. Perhaps my tenacious defensiveness was both an unconscious response to our separation and a necessary part of our separation. Barbara and I have come to understand that our separation was especially strained, difficult, and prolonged because we did not receive appropriate parenting. Our parents fought all the time and were extremely overprotective of us. They were not capable of focusing on the problems that we were having growing up as twins or of parenting us as individuals. In spite of the poor parenting we received, I have always loved Barbara deeply. I think that we had to lead separate lives, that we had to live 500 miles away from each other in order to develop our own careers while raising our children. I think the arguments we had, and there were many, were related in large part to the fact that the intensity of our twin relationship would have interfered with our ability to develop the rich lives that we have as individuals. Perhaps it would have been easier if we had been guided by our parents into a more normal relationship when we were children. We never learned how to compromise as individuals; we knew how to relate if we were a pair but not if we had different goals for ourselves. Our mother always gave us the silent treatment when she was angry, a pattern of relating to each other that has haunted our relationship as adults for many years.

As I write this I realize Barbara has become the more analytical twin in our relationship. This is somewhat ironic. Barbara, who was in our childhood and in college the more emotional twin, has become, in many ways, the more rational twin. Even now, I am the one who carries on the "demon twin" role. I remember fondly pretending to be one of Barbara's "patients" while attending a family dinner in Beverly Hills. I brought my Rollerblades and protective helmet. Barbara just brings out that playfulness in me.

We are busy women. Both of us have full-time careers. I work three-fourths time teaching writing at Stanford University and DeAnza Community College and three-fourths time working on writing textbooks. Barbara, a psychologist, is in her office 40 hours a week and does phone sessions on the weekends with her clients, too, so she was really working overtime to get *Not All Twins Are Alike* done. I honestly don't know how she did it, but I am thankful that she did, and I am enormously proud of her.

Why am I thankful and proud of her? Because I know now that she wanted to help bring us back together by finding out more about the quality of twin relationships by interviewing 30 sets of twins and reflecting on their responses to her questions. Because I know that writing about an issue that troubles you profoundly can help clarify your ideas and feelings and develop a better perspective on your life. As a writing professor, I can say that she found a "shift in perspective" through her writing. This has been an incredibly important transformation for her and for me, and for you, her readers, it is also a striking gift. The twin patterns and the conclusions that she delineates and then supports through case histories are informative, fascinating, and illuminating. *Not All Twins Are Alike* will help you understand what's underneath the double paradox that I wrote of earlier. Barbara goes beyond the surface similarities and differences in the twin pairs she studied to reveal the deeper emotional and intellectual issues that twins have to confront and finally make peace with.

Marjorie Ford, M.A.
Stanford University

Acknowledgments

The 58 adult twins who agreed to speak with me at length about what it was like to grow up with a twin and to work through the problems of fitting into a non-twin world were the crucial cornerstones of this book. I am grateful to these individuals for graciously taking time from their busy lives to speak honestly and enthusiastically about their own sense of being a twin. Their almost immediate responsiveness to my curiosity inspired me to delve more deeply into my own thoughts and feelings about being a twin and how I might help others understand and solve the unique problems that twins confront. I thank these individuals for sharing their life stories with me.

Nita Romer, an acquisitions editor at Praeger, was very interested in my ideas about what is positive and what is negative about the closeness that twins share and how twins are different from normal siblings. Her interest and encouragement motivated me to get started writing a "new" book about twinship. I am very grateful to her for not giving up on my ideas.

Paul Macirowski, another editor and dearest friend, was literally my right-hand man or my twin substitute while I developed my thinking and approach to this book. Paul participated closely on every aspect of this project. His capacity to help me clarify my ideas and feelings about a topic that is very close to my heart was remarkable. His sensitivity to my concerns about being a "freaky twin" were endless. I thank him for first pointing out that he thought that I was acting like my twin sister and not myself, then remaining committed to me and to my book.

Frank Fox, Ph.D., my dear friend and doctoral adviser from 1982, consulted with me on the research design of this book. He read the final draft and helped me make some wise revisions. I am extremely lucky to have had his input.

Arnold Wilson, M.D., my former psychoanalyst, read the final draft of this book and gave me some very useful corrections. I deeply appreciate his feedback about this book.

Finally, I must acknowledge my adult children, Richard and Elizabeth. Because they survived being the children of a twin, they learned a great deal about what "double trouble" twins can really do to your life. Their reactions to me and to their aunt provided the backdrop for this book. I always believed that Richard and Elizabeth would be fascinated with how other non-twins lived through the freaky fun, disasters, dangers, and everyday adventures of their twin relatives. I am continually reminded of their enjoyment of my twin photos, which live on long after we know or care which one is Barbara and which one is Marjorie.

Introduction

Probably since the beginning of human history, twins have been a source of wonder and fascination or of repulsion and fear. Mythologies and religions have used images of twins to convey the meaning and complexity of life. Scientists have used twin research to determine, perhaps incorrectly, what is genetically unalterable in humans. Psychologists have looked at twins and twinship to understand the effect of the environment and caregivers on the development of the individual. Writers, poets, and filmmakers have commonly employed twins to elaborate or dramatize their ideas about the powers of good and evil.

Popular culture often portrays twins as having the ideal intimate relationship. Twins can be viewed as icons of emotional closeness because they serve as mirror images of each other. Supposedly, twins provide a total and complete attentiveness to each other that all individuals consciously or unconsciously long for in relationships. In contrast, unfortunately, twins are also seen in a negative light, as stereotypical freaks, because they are viewed as halves of a whole person or copies of each other.

Recently, twins and parents of twins have begun to question the absurdity and destructiveness that these caricatures of twins embrace, project, and perpetuate. Contemporary writers on twinship are attempting, successfully, to go beyond the idealized or stereotypical images of twinship. They are telling authentic and distinctive life stories of twins. At last, parents of twins are seriously interested in developing individuality in their children. Enlightened parents have stopped focusing on what is cute and special about the similarities between their "double trouble" children. It is hoped that the emphasis on twins as individuals will begin to counteract onlookers' voyeuristic, and double-sided, images of twins as clones of each other and as freaks of nature.

In this book I hope to present a unique perspective on twinship. Twins may look alike, talk alike, and enjoy many of the same activities and friends. However, in spite of all their alikeness, twins are distinct individuals who have shared their mother's womb. All twins who are not separated at birth share the beginning of their lives and their parents' attention and affection more intimately than single children. Identical twins share their genetic endowment, which makes issues of separateness even more complicated and intense. Twins go through developmental milestones together, which creates a need for their co-twin, a need for a twin substitute or close companion, a need for competition and sharing later in life, and a tendency toward feelings of intense loneliness.

Twins have different facets to their sense of self. First, twins are distinct individuals, even though they may look identical and are too often treated as a pair. Second, when twins are together, they develop a sense of self that includes the twin pair as primary. Twins' experiences of being part of a twin pair are quite different than their experiences of not being part of a twin pair. Third, twin identity is complicated by the intensity of their closeness, which twins share and must eventually move away from as they become part of the world outside of their family. Being a twin in a world of non-twins creates misunderstanding and alienation.

Twinship as a unique developmental experience fraught with emotional difficulties and hard-to-attain rewards is ultimately a more fascinating and psychologically meaningful perspective to explore. But who would really want to explore twinship? For a start, twins themselves, parents and relatives of twins, pediatricians, teachers, spouses and children of twins, and mental health counselors who see twins in psychotherapy. And, perhaps, the average inquisitive person.

To gain insight into what it is like to grow up as a twin, I spoke with 30 sets of adult twins, ranging in age from 35 to 88. The majority of twins were in midlife (40 to 60 years old). Fifty-seven percent were identical twins and the others were fraternal twins. These twins came from all walks of life. Teachers, actors, architects, interior designers, landscapers, homemakers, writers, real estate agents and developers, accountants, financial planners, psychologists, social workers, dentists, and contractors shared their experiences growing up as twins. (See Appendix I for a breakdown of the demographic data.)

Each person who agreed to talk with me was referred by someone who had heard of my study, and was seriously interested in sharing his or her experiences of being a twin. Participants came from all over the United States and Canada. I spoke on the phone to people in Quebec, Colorado, Illinois, Hawaii, New Mexico, Massachusetts, North Carolina, Georgia, Ohio, New Jersey, New York, Hawaii, Texas, and Washington. In person I talked to participants in Southern California, where I live.

I wrote a structured interview that appears in Chapter 3. This interview is based on my knowledge and understanding of child and adult development as well as my research on twin development. Each twin was questioned separately for at least one hour. In some instances I spoke with participants for a much longer time, or for two or more occasions, if we thought that more conversation would be useful. Although I did not ask these adult twins not to discuss their answers with their co-twins, most participants told me that they wanted their responses to reflect only their point of view.

In addition to questioning each participant about his or her experience of growing up as a twin, I asked them to contribute their insights about what it meant to be a twin. I tried to glean from twin participants the advantages and disadvantages of sharing so much intimacy with another person. Fortunately, the participants were highly articulate, and each had strong opinions about the effect of twinship upon her or his life choices and overall well-being.

On a more personal level, this book is about the magic and struggles of growing up as a twin. My own life makes me an expert on the subject because I am a twin. I have relished certain experiences with my sister, and I have depended on her in ways that normal sisters cannot imagine. Because of my childhood experiences of being treated as the bad twin, I was ashamed of being a twin for most of my life. Sometimes I wanted a more understandable sister, and for years I wished that I were not a twin, which definitely hurt my sister's feelings. Now I am more resigned to my fate of having spent too many years of my adult life being estranged from my sister and the pain of my loneliness that was created by our distance and alienation. Fortunately, this book has brought us together, but our memories of being alienated from each other are still vivid.

I am interested, perhaps fascinated, in how other twins feel about growing up with a constant companion, who by most standards knows too much about their good and bad points and overall personality qualities, as well as how they look naked or with tailored clothes. I often wonder seriously, "Are twins too close for comfort?"

This book includes my story of growing up as a twin, as well as my sister's story. It is a story of all the twins with whom I spoke during my work on this research project. All our narratives are woven together into a collage of twin tales of development. Our passages through life are, I believe, poignant, funny, bizarre, sad, tragic, magical, and entertaining, and will give others food for thought about longings for intimacy and acceptance.

1

The Ultimate Closeness
Growing Up with Your Mirror Image

THE TIE THAT BINDS

Human longings for closeness, trust, and unconditional companionship are exemplified by images of twins and the fantasy and reality of the ultimate closeness they share. Indeed, our belief that twins share a special kind of intimacy is true, and yet, ironically, it is distorted and misinformed as well. Although it is obvious that twins share more deeply than other sisters and brothers, what is perhaps less apparent is the resentment and anxiety about twinship that diminishes the glory of this supposedly ideal relationship. Understanding more clearly what is valuable about the bond between twins may enlighten others about how to attain closeness and warmth with other people. Twin life experiences can answer the question, "Is it as easy as it seems, to be close and harmonious with another person?" In this book I explore the deep roots of closeness that twins share while shedding light on the true meanings of attachment and intimacy.

Twins do share their early life experiences, which creates an "ultimate closeness." This deeply profound closeness can never be replicated. Naturally, this primary bonding experience creates unique and distinct developmental stages for infants and young twins that strongly affect later development. These distinctive developmental stages are not manifested in the life spans of single children. As important to idiosyncratic twin development are the unique bonding attachments that twins form with each other, which creates special strengths as well as distinct limitations for each member of a twin pair.

The most apparent strength that comes from sharing everything around you—parents, genetics, and environment—is the increased capacity for closeness and sharing, and a deep longing for intimacy. A sense of connectedness, understanding, and trust can ensue. Naturally, as twin infants grow they eagerly enjoy each other's company. Together they welcome others into their emotional world. Twins continue to long for close, intense relationships because having such a relationship was their first and primary experience in life. Singles (less commonly referred to as singletons) often see twins as extremely talented at interacting with others because twins are highly empathic human beings (Schave & Ciriello, 1983).

In contrast to twins' almost magical capacity and need for sharing are distinctive problems with being separate—an inability to set limits for others and a pronounced difficulty being alone. Very early in their lives most twins begin to suffer personality limitations that develop from a lack of separate experiences (Ainslie, 1997; Leonard, 1961). The fearfulness of not being with one's co-twin and an intense need for intimacy creates barriers to each twin's individual psychological development. Understandably and unfortunately, twins have more difficulty than single children learning how to function on their own, without their twin sister or brother. Because they have shared a great deal of time together as infants and young children, twins may have limited skills when communicating with others, including their own parents. Twins also experience more shame, guilt, or confusion about being the center of attention than single-birth individuals, since it is not their preferred way of being.

The legacy of growing up as a twin varies dramatically. Some twins grow up to value and safely rely on the relationship they have with their twin sibling—a relationship built upon deep love and understanding. The legacy for other twins may include a propensity to suffer from profound loneliness or emptiness in situations of isolation from the twin sibling or upon the death of the twin sibling (Woodward, 1998). A dramatic and tragic example was related to me in an interview with a twin whose sister had committed suicide. As we talked, I came to understand how profound and pervasive her loss was. This young woman felt as if she were living with a "hole in her chest" after her sister's death. She was emotionally paralyzed for 10 years after her sister's suicide. But raising four children, participating in successful psychotherapy to deal with her grief, and starting a new career helped her feel almost whole again. Even so, Ann has never been able to completely get over her fear of loss and to develop strong relationships with others besides her children, who are her twin substitutes. (The names in this book have been changed to protect the confidentiality of the participants.)

Other twins who spoke about their twinship confirmed my belief that the emotional support of a twin sister or brother can at times provide and re-create the ultimate closeness of infancy and early childhood—a sense of connectedness, harmony, and well-being that is difficult to attain in even the most intimate adult relationships. Many of these twins had difficult struggles with their twin sibling as adolescents and as adults, but they still thought they could glean some special understanding and hope from each other. The psychological issues of missing one's sibling and of separation between siblings clearly have different meanings for twins than for single children because of twins' shared experiences.

UNRAVELING THE TIE THAT BINDS

Giving up the ultimate closeness and comfort that twinship provides is a process that begins at birth. Parents provide the most crucial direction for their children's overall abilities to form their own identities separate from, but related to, their twin identity. By their conscious and unconscious interactions and responses to their twin children, parents lay the foundation for each child's capacity for an integrated and complete personality (Burlingham, 1952, 1963; Schave, 1982). For example, parents who are overwhelmed and indifferent to their twin children's special needs may not be attentive enough to see differences between their twins. Overwhelmed parents may feel comfortable treating their twins as if they are copies of each other. Other parents can be inattentive in a different way. These parents will quickly lay down arbitrary distinctions between their twins. For instance, one is the prized child and the other is the difficult one, the stereotypical "bad seed." Of course, no child is all good or all bad, but these anxious and rigid parents see what they want to and respond to their own inner voices. Attentive parents seriously try to see how their infants are unique individuals.

Depending on the quality of parenting twins receive, they are more or less at risk for being overly dependent on each other's personality strengths and limitations—their psychic structure. Many of the twins I spoke with reported that they were treated by their parents as a "unit joined at the hip." Obviously, undifferentiated young twins may feel incomplete without each other. They need the presence of the other twin to finish their sentences, tie their shoes, stop crying, or go to sleep. Twins who were treated as polar opposites of each other established roles and rules for who did what for whom, but they have serious dependency and self-image issues. In more optimal situations, where individuality was valued, twins enjoy sharing and their companionship with each other, which provides a lifelong bond of understanding.

Adequately parenting twins involves a focus on developing uniqueness and independence in each child (Malmstrom & Poland, 1999). When there is limited or inadequate parenting, one twin can assume the more dominant role, whereas the other is more passive and submissive. This overly dependent interaction can be functional when twins are infants and very young children. Twins' incomplete personalities—their diffusion of identities—become dysfunctional and behaviorally problematic as verbal, social, and educational pressures require twins to separate from each other.

In this chapter I discuss what is unique about early twin development and the special pressures and demands of parenting twins. Specifically, early bonding experiences between parents and twins create sensitivities and limitations that non-twin children do not experience. As a result, twins have difficulties with self-expression, language acquisition, and social understanding as infants and young children that carry over into their adult lives with both positive and negative repercussions (Burlingham, 1952; Koch, 1966; Malmstrom & Poland, 1999; Schave, 1982; Schave & Ciriello, 1983). Because parents are the critical determinants of the early life, I cover parenting styles first. Then I describe how early memories, self-concept, social skills, and unique self-esteem issues are expressed and played out in childhood. Life examples are presented to highlight the unique aspects of growing up with a twin.

When using personal pronouns to refer to a mythical, generic twin, I violate APA style guidelines and somewhat randomly choose "he" or "she," but not both, to avoid the awkwardness of "they" and "he/she."

PARENTS OF TWINS: LAYING THE FOUNDATION FOR PERSONALITY DEVELOPMENT

Twins are fascinating subjects for psychological researchers because they provide a way to understand the genetic components of identity compared with environmental effects. Identical twins are compared with fraternal twins in discrete measures of personality and physical characteristics. When identical twins are found to be more similar than fraternal twins, the trait is considered to be determined by genetic endowment. When there is no difference between identical and fraternal twins on a discrete measure, the trait is considered to be determined by environmental influences. Twin studies have taught us that intelligence, cognitive capacity, and personality characteristics such as introversion, temperament, and sociability have strong genetic components. Physical characteristics such as height, weight, eye color, and propensity to disease processes are also inherited, according to twin research (Segal, 1999).

Parenting as an environmental determinant of infant and child development is also the focus of twin research (Schave & Ciriello, 1983). Twin studies that include parents are limited, but indicate that parents are crucial to the child's emotional and cognitive well-being. The interviews with adult twins that make up this research confirm previous attempts to understand the parents' role in development, because the twins interviewed directly suggested that their parents were crucial in defining differences between them, which led to the development of their adult identity.

What was curious to me in terms of the parents' role in development was how twins remember themselves within their families, because these memories seem to be windows to parental attitudes and styles. Understandably, there is a great deal of variation in how twins in a pair remember their early childhood. Some twins remember playing in their cribs or playpens contentedly, whereas others have more stressful early memories, such as getting into trouble together. This variation in memory retention suggests the dominant influence of parenting on development. All of the twins with whom I spoke reported, without hesitation, their earliest memory as being part of a twin pair, which indicates the primary nature of the twinning bond. Memories of being a single individual without a twin came later in life. From my 20 years of experience doing psychodynamic psychotherapy, single children's earliest memories are of themselves alone, without a sister or brother (Schave & Ciriello, 1983).

Early memories that reflected the comfort and attention related to being a twin included the following: "I remember playing happily in the sandbox together," and "I remember the comfort of lying next to my sister in our cribs." "I remember walking to the park with my sister, hand in hand." "I remember climbing up and down the backyard fence, encouraging each other to go faster."

Other early memories that twins shared with me suggest self-consciousness about being a twin. Many of the twins I spoke with reported, "I remember being 'the twins' and other people staring at us and asking, 'Are they twins?'"

Memories from my own life include a story repeatedly told by family members of how my clever older brother tied a large red sign to our joined-together strollers that said in bold letters, "YES, THEY ARE TWINS." This sign, he hoped, would eliminate what he saw as needless questions about his attention-getting and overwhelming twin sisters. But my brother's sign was just a stopgap measure that could not quell his anger and disappointment at being displaced as the center of attention in our family. Other twins in this study reported that their siblings were strongly affected—either positively or negatively—by their births and the attention given to them as twins. Interestingly and understandably, the twins in this study indicated that the birth of a single brother or sister did not have as dramatic an effect as the birth of twins on the family.

It was not uncommon for the twins I interviewed to suggest that they found the attention they received for being twins quite disturbing. One twin told me about her memory of her first day in kindergarten.

After school one of the kindergarten mothers was talking to my mother. This loud and obnoxious woman told my helpless, befuddled mother about how her daughter Janey was excited that she had seen two girls who looked just like each other sitting next to her on the rug. Janey said to her mother, 'There is a girl with two heads in kindergarten.' My mother thought Janey had never seen twins before. For my mother this was a funny story, so she spread it around to relatives, friends, and neighbors. Meanwhile, this funny little story left an indelible mark on us. We felt like we were the girl with two heads. The message was that we were freaks when we were together.

"'A walking side show on four legs' is my strongest memory of growing up as a twin," reported Cindy, whose mother used her children to get attention from others. As adults Cindy and Debbie feel very awkward when they are together.

Another telling early memory story suggests the strength of a mother's identification with her twin children's appearance. Fraternal twin boys Peter and Raymond recalled being dropped off for the school bus in kindergarten. "My mother, in her own exuberant style, said to the bus driver, 'Take care of my twins.' The bus driver, a bit of a know-it-all himself, said to my mom, 'These boys are not twins. They are just brothers.' The school bus was late for kindergarten because my mom and the bus driver fought over whether or not we were twins. It was a humiliating experience for us—even though we really liked being twins."

Another early memory that was unique and revealing was recollected by Candy, who was terminally ill with cancer at the time I spoke with her. She recalled playing with matches with her fraternal twin sister in the backyard. Candy and Serena, at the age of four and a half, managed to light the matches and start a fire in their backyard. Fortunately, their mother found the girls and prevented the house from catching on fire. Serena and Candy were punished for their dangerous behavior. Serena reported a different and less troubled early memory of playing in the sandbox together. I believe that Candy's memory of the fire the girls started is more ominous and frightening because she was so close to death at the time I spoke with her.

Natalie and Veronica, identical twins who lived through World War II together, reported their first memory at the German front. "I remember always wanting to be with my sister." "I remember singing and dancing together at performances for the soldiers." Today Veronica and Natalie live in the same city and work together in the film industry.

Greg and Julie, fraternal twins, recalled a story of competition as their earliest memory. "Julie and I would leave school at the same time and race home together. She would get home first and I would cry because I was last," Greg said. As adults Julie and Greg still share a very competitive relationship, which is often based on who makes the rules of the game, metaphorically speaking.

Identical twins Kevin and Kyle recalled their father feeding them pretzels in their high chairs. "Father would tease me," said Kevin. "He wouldn't tease my brother." Kevin, who was more alienated from his father and closer to his mother, later realized he is gay.

Memories that twins reported indicate that the type of bond they share is determined early in their life. Early memories were highly predictive of later attachment patterns between twins (Schave & Ciriello, 1983). Memories that twins reported underscore that the outcome of raising twins is complicated by their genetic similarities and the reality of simultaneous development. Twins may look alike and act very similarly, which causes other people to stare at them. But fortunately, and unequivocally, what we know about twin development indicates that the genetic blueprint of life does not override the importance of parenting and of the twin bond itself—the consequence of human interactions. Twin studies show the significance of what is inherited and unalterable, such as blue eyes and blond hair. But twin studies also show how important early interventions can be—specifically, parenting.

The twins with whom I spoke at length helped me understand just how crucial parenting can be in determining who people become as they move through their lives. Parenting provides the substance that molds and holds together what human beings inherit and what can be changed by environmental stimulation.

RAISING TWINS: A CHALLENGE FOR CAREGIVERS

Most emphatically, raising twins to be individuals is very difficult. It requires insight and empathy, a capacity for self-reflection, and a lot of energy. As I have said previously, raising twins as a unit is a recipe for psychological disaster. Ideally, parents should respond to what differences they perceive, rather than create arbitrary distinctions between their twins. Although this is an easy concept to understand, finding and responding to real rather than perceived differences between twins can be extremely tricky and difficult.

Imagine the following scenario—a composite of the stories of the twins with whom I spoke:

Beatrice (T1) and Maggie (T2) have been home from the hospital for several weeks. They still look almost exactly alike. Although Maggie has a small birthmark on her face that helps to tell them apart, it is not always the focus of attention when the household is hectic—which is all the time now that the girls are home. They are still wearing their blue and white hospital bracelets, labeled T1 and T2, which is the only way that caretakers can quickly identify one twin from the other. The bracelets are necessary to prevent any more confusion in an already overwhelmed home. Beatrice, T1, is three minutes older than her sister, Maggie.

Beatrice and Maggie are most comfortable lying next to each other in their crib or baby carriage, but it is not always possible to keep the girls next to each other. The babies need to be changed and fed almost every three hours because they are very small. Feeding the girls is stressful because Mom thinks she has to feed them together to keep them from crying. She really does not know what to do about their crying, which causes the family to be on edge. Mom looks to her own mother and many sisters for help, which causes a different and new problem in the house: too many solutions.

Being the mother of twins provides two distinct challenges. First, the mother and other caregivers have to find real differences between their twin children. Second, mothers need to learn to deal with the closeness that twins share. Beatrice and Maggie calm each other down by being close to each other, as they were in the womb. The calming or soothing presence of their mother has to be developed and established—in essence, added to the relationship that the twins already share with each other. This unique developmental stage is not a problem with single-birth children, who do not have anyone to turn to for comfort but their mother or other primary caregiver. But mother often has to compete with her twins to become a significant emotional support. Early in the life of her twins, mom's role of significance is feeding and changing her children and making sure they are not cold or overheated. Calming and soothing is a nonverbal or preverbal experience between twins, which can go unnoticed and get intertwined if mother is harassed, preoccupied, or unsure of herself. Mother has to compete with the calming presence of the twin.

Let's go back to our imaginary twins, who are now eight months old.

Beatrice and Maggie are sitting up and playing happily together in their playpen. They have been given many toys by friends and relatives. Some were specifically for Beatrice and some were specifically for Maggie. The girls really don't care if their toys get mixed up. They seem to enjoy sharing their dolls, stuffed animals, plastic keys, and teething rings. Maggie looks at her baby bear, puts it in her mouth, and then hands it to Beatrice, who is also interested in tasting their bear. For 30 peaceful minutes the girls play happily. Mom and everyone else who is home is thankful for this quiet break. Last night both girls were up for three hours because they are teething. Just as Beatrice stopped crying and went to sleep, Maggie would wake up in pain and start to cry. There was no way to get both children to stay asleep at the same time.

Mom is tired of dealing with both girls at once, so she has very little interest in treating each child as a unique individual. Although Mom can tell her girls apart and has taken off their name bracelets, everyday problems of care and feeding are still a high priority. Beatrice and Maggie are treated as a unit more often than their mom would like to admit—it is just easier to have the twins entertain each other. It is actually very difficult to separate the girls and give them their own special "alone" time.

Mom has talked to a few friends who have twins about how frustrated she is when she can't settle the girls down. Even her pediatrician has tried to reassure her that these are normal difficulties for twins, but she still feels insecure as a mother. She even feels left out of the loop of love and companionship between Beatrice and Maggie.

Parents of twins have a serious and unique problem to contend with as they compete with the closeness that young twins share. Parents have to work to develop a special attachment to each child. It is very common for twins to prefer each other's company over that of their mother or father. Perhaps this provokes a need for attention-seeking behavior that some parents thrive on when people make a fuss over their twins. In other words, when mothers and fathers don't get as much attention as they want from their twins, they crave the secondary uplift of hearing, "Your twins are so cute."

Onlookers are often mesmerized by twins to the point of absurdity. But if a mother of twins is tired, frustrated, or feeling inadequate, any kind of positive input feels good. The mother most likely doesn't have the courage or even the energy to ask onlookers to stop staring at and comparing her children. At first, onlookers are harmless observers, but as time goes by, mother and twins get used to this public image of the pair. It becomes all too natural for mother and twins to answer the ridiculous, intrusive questions of, "Who is stronger, smarter, happier?" ad nauseam. The public image that twins acquire creates problems for the development of their individual identities. In addition, it can make each of them self-conscious about being a twin.

PARENTING STYLES AND PATTERNS OF TWINSHIP

The public image of twinship and the early bond that twins share are definite problems that single children do not have to cope with or resolve later in life

(Malmstrom & Poland, 1999; Pearlman & Ganon, 2000). Quite simply stated, single children, no matter how close they may be, do not have to simultaneously share their mother's and father's love and attention. Single children do not have issues with identity formation because of very distinctive developmental time alone with each parent, as well as the parents' clarity about who is who and which child needs what.

The resolution of these identity issues related to identity confusion are based on the quality of parenting that twins receive. How do parents deal with onlookers asking, "Are they twins?" How do parents separate their twins and help them become individuals? In my earlier research with adult twins I found that the parents' capacity to see differences between their twins created the nature of their twinning bond, which endured throughout their lives. During this earlier research, I found six distinct types of twinning bonds that I call patterns of twinship (Schave & Ciriello, 1983). In my current research I found four patterns of twinship (see Table 1.1 for a brief summarizing description).

Unit identity was found in twins whose identity was shared in such a way that they could not exist without each other. Parenting of these twins was extremely limited and psychologically abusive. Life trauma was present in infancy or early childhood. These twins exhibited a relationship that is reminiscent of the relationship among children raised in wartime concentration camps (Bowlby, 1958). Just as these unfortunate orphans of World War II turned to each other to be surrogate parents, unit identity twins turned to each other. From each other they received physical comfort, a degree of psychological security, and a constant, trustworthy presence. Their lack of parenting created an extreme dependency upon each other. Indeed, these twins had a traumatically caused symbiotic tie. Because of the lack of parenting that these twins received, they created differences between themselves in an attempt to feel separateness and to deal with the demands of the outer world (Farber, 1981). Twins with a unit identity are able to live productive lives, but they seem to have intense difficulty forming relationships with others. They are reluctant to marry, and if they do, the marriages are short-lived. Unit identity twins are unable to survive emotionally without their co-twin.

Twins who develop an interdependent identity clearly say that their co-twin is more important to them than their parents. The parenting these types of twins received was very limited. Although these twins were not traumatically abused or neglected as with unit identity twins, there was a lack of positive experiences from parents, who were either hostile or indifferent to their children. In most of these twinships, parents were burdened or disappointed by their twin children. In reaction to feeling unloved by their parents, these twins became very involved with the love and acceptance of their twin. The twin bond in part replaced the parent-child bond, which served to intensify the need for closeness between the twins. Eventual separation from each other is very difficult. These twins usually marry people who can accept their twin sister or brother. They choose very similar or the same careers and have no apparent need to form friendships outside of their relationship. Because their parents

Table 1.1
Patterns of Twinship

Patterns of Twinship	Parenting Received	Personality Characteristics
Unit Identity	Very minimal but abusive parenting, along with traumatic life circumstances such as living through World War II	Extreme co-dependency between twins
		Lack of deep relationships outside of twinship
		Separation and individuation never attained
Interdependent Identity	Limited parenting that is abusive, hostile, or indifferent	Co-dependent relationship between twins
		Trust twin above all other relationships
		Twin always a part of deep relationships
Split Identity	Parents establish contrived differences between twins	Highly conflicted relationship with twin
	Schizophrenogenic mother	Shame about being a twin
		Carefully establish trusting relationships with others
		Hold on to label of the "bad" one or "good" one as an adult
Individual Identity	Parents respond to real differences between twins	Close, intense attachment to twin
	Emphasis on individuality	Form strong attachments outside of twinship
	Respect for twin bond	Twin is trusted best friend

have not made distinctions between them, they create differences between themselves that they can tolerate despite such closeness (Farber, 1981).

Split identity was another pattern of twinship that I was able to identify in both my earlier and my current research. Twins who have a split identity twinship have received positive feelings from their parents for being twins. Their parents are usually very excited about having twins because of the special attention their children attract from other people. The parents are very aware of the differences between their children, in part because they focus on their similarities. Unfortunately, these twins do not receive adequate individual attention. Differences between these twin children are based on how the mother perceives that her children are different rather than on real distinctions. One twin is the container for the mother's positive sense of herself; the other twin, her negative sense of herself. Obviously, this type of parenting comes from a mother who has unresolved emotional issues and cannot deal with her own mixed feelings about her children and the work of child rearing. Splitting her twins into "good" and "bad" is the mother's way of dealing with her frustration and confusion.

The split identity bond burdens twins because their interdependence is conflicted rather than harmonious, as with unit identity twins and interdependent identity twins. The good twin in the split gets sick of taking care of her bad twin sister, who in turn tires of being measured as less than her good twin sister. A lot of shameful feelings are related to this twin bond. Fortunately, split identity twins go their separate ways as teenagers in order to form relationships that are based on more realistic assessments of who they really are as individuals. But these twins hang on to the labels they received as young children, which creates problems with their individual self-esteem. The good twin develops grandiose expectations for herself, whereas the bad twin has great difficulty holding on to what is positive about her personality.

Individual identity twins are raised to be individuals. Parenting, although difficult for these mothers, is not overwhelming. The parents may focus on how cute their twins are, but they also focus on what is distinctive about each child. They respect the bond between their twins but also directly encourage individuality. Individual identity twins are exhorted and expected to be able to function without their twin sibling. Because these twins are aware that they are separate people who are similar, they tend to measure themselves against each other as well as to support each other when their co-twin falls behind or needs help. Individual development in infancy and early childhood allows these twins to function on their own very successfully in their careers and in relationships (Schave & Ciriello, 1983).

Fraternal boy-girl twins fall into the individual identity pattern. Parents of these children treat them differently because of apparent sexual differences, which creates developmental distinctiveness. These boy-girl twins are very closely linked as children but develop unique identities as adults. Their sense of themselves as twins diminishes as they grow older, which is in strong contrast to single-sex twins.

Patterns of twinship based on parenting styles endure throughout the lives of twins. Within these patterns there can still be different individual twin relationships. But across the patterns of twinship there is a closeness that came from sharing childhood experiences that is more intense than between single children who are close together in age.

THE UNTOLD STORY: EARLY LIFE EXPERIENCES

All twins are socialized differently than single children because they have each other, which is usually more than enough interpersonal experience when they are infants and toddlers. As they start preschool and kindergarten, twins are exposed to other children, who relate to them as part of a pair or as individuals. The capacity to form new social relationships is related to the twins' early experiences with others. The more experience twins have with other people besides their twin, the easier it is for them to act independently.

The twins I interviewed for this study were not isolated from other children or siblings as infants and young children. Overall, as children they shared friends as they had shared toys and clothes when they were younger. One adult twin explained quite eloquently what she saw as the problem of understanding the early childhood experiences of twins: "Because of the nature of their intense closeness growing up—shared language, feelings, and experiences—twins have a great deal of difficulty explaining the experience of twinship as an infant and young child to others." This inability to explain themselves to others is related to the reality that twins spend so much time together that they do not necessarily want to learn to explain themselves to others. As twins grow up they lack the motivation and intellectual and emotional capacity to verbalize their privately shared relationship with new people. Oftentimes their untold story is lost or inaccurately presented by others who fixate on the outward appearances of twins. Early life experiences of twins are misunderstood and misperceived by single individuals.

School Experiences

Most of the twins with whom I spoke came from families who realized that their children needed to begin to be separated when they started kindergarten. Whether or not parents were psychologically minded, i.e., insightful and empathic to their children's struggle, they knew enough to understand the limitations of closeness and sharing; they realized that their children needed to develop individual strengths outside of their home lives. This transition to broadening their social world in school created some minor obstacles that needed to be overcome. For example, shy twins had trouble explaining their thoughts, feelings, and ideas to other children and to teachers. They preferred doing schoolwork with their twin rather than other classmates. Even these shy twins were able to adjust to working with other children, though, because teachers expected them to interact academically and socially without their twin. Parents of twins also encouraged their children to master school situations as individuals. The twins I questioned enjoyed meeting other children at school and at extracurricular activities, such as music, sports, dance lessons, and Girl or Boy Scouts. Gradually, they formed new friendships with other children, which expanded their social world.

DEVELOPING A SENSE OF SELF IN CHILDHOOD

Dressing Alike

As children, twins always have to deal with their twin identity. A twin is always just himself as well as half of a twin pair. This, of course, complicates his social sense of self and his self-concept. To try to understand how a twin dealt with his private self and public self, I was interested in how the twins I interviewed remembered and felt about dressing alike or dressing differently. I believe that, for twins, outward appearance has a special meaning that is directly related to how they want to be perceived by others. Every twin I spoke with had answers to my questions about dressing alike.

Very few of the twins I spoke with dressed differently as young children. I would guess that about 80% of this sample of twins dressed alike until second or third grade. Some twins dressed alike until eighth grade. The two sets of twins who were over 70 years old dressed alike until they attended college, which suggests that there was a definite social and cultural trend toward developing individuality in twins by dressing them differently between the years 1930 and 1965. In other words, the younger members of this sample were dressed differently much earlier than the older twins.

As adolescents, twins wanted to dress differently. They continued to share their clothes but they were very careful not to be seen together wearing the same outfit. In fact, most twins at this time in their lives tried to develop new styles for themselves that made them feel like they were very distinct individuals. For example, one twin might select a preppie style, whereas her sister chose a more bohemian style. The male twins I spoke with were not as interested in clothing issues as the female twins, who really enjoyed sharing clothes or dressing in outfits that complemented each other. Perhaps male twins are similar to males in the general population and do not enjoy clothing as much as females.

Later in life female twins liked to share clothes with each other or trade outfits to expand their wardrobes. I believe that sharing and trading clothes is a positive way for twins to connect with the closeness of childhood. Even twins who were brought up to be individuals and were encouraged to dress differently did not object to sharing their clothes. In fact, I was surprised to find that dressing alike was not an issue or point of conflict for twins. Rather, dressing alike or in a similar manner was something they liked to do because it made them feel proud of themselves and of one another.

Sharing Center Stage

Not all of the twins I spoke to liked to be asked if they were twins. Some thought that being stared at was freaky or annoying. Some twins enjoyed the extra attention they got from onlookers. But all the twins I questioned seemed to enjoy being twins. As young children they were not self-conscious about the similarities in physical appearance, thought patterns, speech patterns, and voice intonation that they shared. The quality of parenting they received was not projected on to their conscious sense of themselves as children. They were not concerned about other people's perceptions of themselves as individuals. In fact most twins I spoke with shared their early photographs with me. None of the photographs I saw were of single children. The twins who talked with me were fascinated with being twins. They held on to memories of their twinship in their own minds and through photographs. Clearly, being a twin in childhood was a positive experience that generated a lot of pride.

Although not all of the twins with whom I spoke could articulate or cared to articulate the closeness and companionship they shared as children, it was apparent to me that having a constant friend and colleague for fun, trouble-making, or outsmarting parents and teachers was a definite advantage. A sense of friendship and a feeling of trust because one had a twin with whom to share good and bad experiences offset any problems this kind of across-the-board sharing might bring for non-twin brothers or sisters. For example, it would be hard to persuade two sisters to share a best friend. Young twins, on the other hand, could understand the value of sharing a friend. This positive attitude toward sharing uniquely and profoundly shapes the early life of twins. Sharing creates a unique bond between the pair. In addition, the belief that sharing is a natural and acceptable way to behave with other people leads to unique socialization patterns.

The Twin As a Competitor

Most of the twins I spoke with confirmed there was a strong competitive aspect to their relationship that was manifested in childhood. Competition between twins had different functions. Because young twins and school-age twins are so used to sharing, competition was often seen as a game. It was common for school-age twins to measure themselves against each other as a way of establishing their identities as a distinct part of the twin pair. The "compare and contrast" game was constant, creating playfulness along with anger and disappointment when not measuring up to the other.

Competition between twins was adaptive because it helped them define the individual strengths and limitations of each twin. It also helped them see that they were their own distinct person. Competition was never cutthroat or a "do or die" type of experience. In split identity twinship, competition was used to define one twin as the smarter, stronger, or more attractive twin. In other patterns of twinship, competition manifested itself as dominance and non-dominance: the winner was dominant and the loser was non-dominant. Dominance was always alternating between the twins in the pair, which made competition a style of interacting rather than a final outcome or event.

In adolescence twins rebelled against being compared and contrasted with each other. This rebellion changed the rules of the game of compare and contrast. Teenage twins became angry at continually being measured against each other and started defining themselves outside the twinship. Teenagers tried to take up totally separate interests, friends, and clothing in order to experiment with just being themselves. The need to establish a separate identity outside of being a twin continued into adulthood.

The Power of Twinship: Double Trouble

The adult twins I interviewed all enjoyed using their twinship to create confusion, play tricks, or get special attention. Perhaps this was a way to get back at the onlookers in their childhoods who asked ridiculous, intrusive, and inappropriate questions. This power began in toddlerhood, or as soon as twins could understand that there was more power in two than in one, and continued well into adolescence. Creating double trouble is unique to twinship and was fondly remembered in adulthood.

Separate Interests and Separate Friends

Most of the twins I spoke with began to develop their own friends and special interests as soon as they began to go to school. Parents were important as motivators for separate experiences. Most "good enough" parents tried to have their own special times and interests with each of their twin children. A twin's separate interests, along with different tastes in friends, continued to develop in conjunction with a close relationship with his or her twin sibling. Adolescence brought a greater number of distinctive interests and choices for friendships. Still, there was a great deal of closeness and consultation with the twin sibling as a normal part of growing up and growing apart.

CONCLUSIONS

Twins share an ultimate closeness at birth, throughout infancy, and into childhood that is based on growing up together and sharing parents and the home environment. This profound closeness is gradually loosened as twins develop distinct identities, with conscious and unconscious input from their parents, as well as through countless interactions with each other.

As young twins go out into the world, they have each other to rely on when they feel overwhelmed or stressed. In addition, they have their parents to look to for direction and support.

The childhood experiences twins share are their most memorable and intense. All the twins with whom I spoke had positive thoughts and feelings about having a full-time companion and trustworthy friend. Because twins had someone who could completely understand and empathize with their experiences, traumatic events and everyday upsetting situations at school or with parents were more tolerable. A twin is a buffer—someone with whom to share the pain, someone to absorb part of the misery, et cetera. And, yes, someone to share the thrill of learning how to read, how to ice-skate, how to pull an engine block and machine the heads.

Serious self-esteem issues were not reported to have surfaced in childhood among the group of twins who spoke with me. Twinship seemed to enhance these young children's sense of self-worth and competence. Oftentimes these twins used their alikeness to model, perform on stage, dance, or compete in sports activities. Companionship seemed to bolster their good feelings about their experiences in life. Even competition between twins could be a positive expression of differences, an outlet for twins who were often compared and contrasted. Some twins used their talents to succeed in an arena, both literally and metaphorically, without their twin sibling. Or they competed side by side, cheering each other on.

Issues of separation can be apparent in early childhood, when one twin cries because he misses his brother. School-age twins learn to have separate experiences in the classroom, but more often than not turn to each other for advice and support with schoolwork and friends. The capacity to tolerate longer separations from each other appears in later childhood, when twins go off to camp separately or spend time with different relatives. At this point in their lives, twins are able to get through many days without each other.

As childhood comes to a close, the intense need for the twin is greatly diminished. Twins eagerly start adolescence with lots of energy and the determination to make their individual mark on the world, without their twin. Outwardly, or to the untrained eye, twins appear to have gotten over their intense attachment to each other.

2

Separation
A Crucial Formative Experience

PARENTAL DETERMINANTS OF THE SEPARATION PROCESS

Psychoanalytic intellectuals have described the process of separation between a mother and her child as a profound, complicated, and ongoing experience (Erickson, 1950, 1968; Mahler, 1967; Stern, 1985). Although the inter-twin relationship has not been as thoroughly analyzed as the mother-child relationship, psychoanalysts have theorized that the separation process between twins is as intense and complicated as the separation experience between a mother and child (Burlingham, 1952). A mother of twins and her twins go through two distinctive separations. The separation processes between mother and child and between the twins themselves are intertwined and proceed through a series of stages that build upon one another.

The basic foundation of the personality, other than the genetic blueprint, is developed out of the quality of attachment between mother and child. As with any foundation, be it a house or person, the initial underlying structure provides the stability for future growth and development. With good enough attention to an infant or young child's needs for security, trust, and autonomy, the foundation for the child's capacity to separate from mother and family is thus constructed (Winnicott, 1960, 1970). Without a strong and secure foundation, based on the mother's attention to and toleration for the true self of her infant, future growth will be inhibited, arrested, or totally retarded (Miller, 1981; Socarides & Stolorow, 1984–85). As parents attend to their infant's basic needs for food, care, and love, the infant grows more competent and self-reliant, and she is able to tolerate more separate experiences from her caregivers. She slowly learns to feed herself and move around on her own. This developmental process continues to unfold exponentially and reciprocally. Parents nurture their children, and as they grow up, they branch out to find others who will also nurture them and help them develop or expand themselves (Ainsworth, 1974; Bell, 1977; Kohut, 1977; Socarides & Stolorow, 1984–85).

Twin development is more complicated than single-child development. Twins have each other to turn to for attention, comfort, and emotional support. This primary and primitive bond with each other develops in parallel to the mother-child bond. A sense of physical separateness from each other gradually develops as twins crawl, then walk. Very slowly, infant twins begin to experience themselves as two separate people. Research suggests that just-born infant twins most likely are not aware that their hand is separate from their twin's hand. This initial oneness creates a very intense attachment, where connection and sharing are totally natural states of being, and separateness is an atypical experience (Malmstrom & Poland, 1999).

The mother's presence initially physically separates her twins. If we return to Beatrice (T-1) and Maggie (T-2), we remember that they cry uncontrollably when mom tries to feed them separately. In spite of all their fussing, though, gradually these infant twins are able to tolerate some physical separation from each other. Although young twins prefer to be in each other's company as much as possible, they need to learn to function as separate people. The mother negotiates her twin children's capacity to grow apart and to become independent identities. The mother's first task in separating her twins is to find distinctions between them. Sometimes the mother perceives physical differences first, such as a birthmark on one but not the other. Emotional differences are an additional way that the mother can view her children as distinct. One twin will be more temperamental; the other twin will be calm. It may be difficult to find the exact characteristics the mother uses to make distinctions between her children. However, whatever focus the mother uses to differentiate between her children, it is the act of defining individuality based on observable differences that is crucial.

In most cases where mothers are emotionally stable, they can observe individual differences between their twin children. Unfortunately, when mothers are overwhelmed by parenting twins, they often do not distinguish between them. Instead, they treat their twins as if they were a singular unit. When twin children lack input from the mother that they are different from each other, they can become overly attached to each other. In these situations, the mother is remembered as cold and indifferent by her twins. Twins with mothers who were overwhelmed by the circumstances of twin birth or an emotional illness clearly remember being treated as a "unit joined at the hip." They cannot recall how their mother treated them differently. The mother's lack of a distinctive and individual connection to each twin creates enormous stress for the twin attachment, which becomes parentified. These types of twins have a double attachment—they are twins as well as surrogate parents to each other. Overly attached twins find separation from their mother insignificant and separation from their twin impossible. Their connection to each other is so intertwined that they need each other to function. They remain best of friends throughout their lives, but they are never as comfortable being close to other people as they are with their twin sibling.

Many mothers are not detached from their twin children, but still have a great deal of difficulty establishing substantial attachments with them. These types of mothers enjoy having twins and the attention that their children bring to themselves and their family. Yet these emotionally unstable, arbitrary, and rigid mothers are unable to deal with the confusion of raising twins. They do not treat their children as an amorphous unit; rather, they label each twin as if they were half of a whole person. The good twin, who can do no wrong, and the bad twin, who can do nothing right, result from this type of faulty perception and unjustified labeling.

Speculatively speaking, this split identity occurs because the mother needs to contain the demands of parenting. Twins who are perceived to have a fixed identity are less confusing to deal with for a mother who has difficulty setting limits for herself and her children. Attachment and separation from the schizophrenogenic mother and her split identity twins are perverted, or distorted. The attachment and eventual separation process between mother and bad twin is built upon depression and neglect—the mother ignores the bad twin because of her own desperate sadness and sense of hopelessness about her future. The attachment between mother and good twin is based on grandiosity and permissiveness. Without a doubt, the bond between these twins is seriously conflicted.

Split identity twins can exist for each other only when they are "half of a whole person." Together they can function as a psychic unit because one twin takes the blame and the other takes the fame. When these twins separate, they have to face the reality that they feel a great deal of anger and resentment toward each other. They have been emotionally burdened by having to complement each other, yet they feel dissatisfied and incomplete when apart. Anger at each other is manifested as criticism, because the good twin is ashamed of her twin and the bad twin is ashamed of herself. Split identity twins also resent their parents for not treating them as individuals. These twins separate from their parents in a very different manner than the other twins described.

Split identity twins become aware of their troubled hostile relationship in adolescence. The twinship provides a comfort and companionship in childhood, but as these twins grow apart, they find that being separate is much easier than being together. Initial separation as infants and young children is stressful for these twins, but adolescent separation is a welcome relief. Emily, an identical twin with a split identity, described twinship as a curse. Mary and Melinda, also identical split identity twins, have had a troubled relationship since the age of 20. They have bitter fights with each other and avoid each other as much as possible. For 20 years they were completely estranged.

Twins who have a substantial individual attachment to the mother develop a strong and resilient attachment to each other. Unlike interdependent identity twins, whose lives remain intertwined and enmeshed, or split identity twins, who have a difficult time being together after their initial separation, twins who have a strong and functional attachment to their mother also have a strong and functional relationship with each other. Twins who have received good enough parenting are able to separate from each other. They are able to tolerate being together as well as being separate as older children and as adults.

All of the twins I interviewed who were treated as individuals by their parents were positive that their parents were able to distinguish between them at birth. These parents were psychologically minded enough to look for and develop real distinctions between their identical or fraternal twin children. Whether or not these children wore their identification bracelets from the hospital for many months, their mothers had a good sense of emotional differences as well as physical differences. These mothers also seemed to be sensitive to the closeness and special nature of their bond. Attention was paid to learning unique aspects of twin development, such as competitiveness, and the pitfalls of making comparisons between twin children. Because of the inherent psychological nature of this type of parenting, separation issues between twins themselves and between twins and their parents seemed to be more manageable. These parents communicated non-verbally, as well as verbally, with their young twins about being separated from each other. One adult twin I spoke with reported, "When we started kindergarten, mother told us that separation from one another was going to be very hard, but there was no way we could understand just how hard it was for us not to be together."

Individuality as an important attribute of personality was stressed, which facilitated the eventual separation process. Parents did not leave separation issues for their children to cope with alone, and they were sensitive to problems that evolved from too much closeness between twins. One adult twin told me, "My father wanted us to be in separate classrooms so that we could develop our own strengths and learn to be on our own." Other twins reported that their parents dealt with developing their individuality by letting them make as many of their own choices as were practical. For example, identical twin girls, five years old, were allowed to choose clothing from their own dressers.

See Table 2.1 for a review of twins' separation experiences.

SOCIAL TRENDS TOWARD ENCOURAGING SEPARATION AND INDIVIDUALITY

When I was growing up in the 1950s, my parents followed the accepted child-rearing folklore that twins were special and cute and should be treated as a pair. Unquestionably, my family and many other families of the 1940s and 1950s did not question this absurdity and fostered the closeness that twinship provides. My sister and I, like many other twins with whom I spoke, were inseparable. We shared a special language, and we shared our friends and all our possessions. There was very little emphasis on developing individuality in twins before 1970. In this study, the older the twins, the less likely that individuality was stressed. Two sets of over-70-year-old twins were allowed to dress alike until they entered college.

Table 2.1
Separation Capacity

Pattern of Twinship	Intensity of Stress during Separations	Resolution of Separation
Unit Identity	Overwhelming	No separation from twin
Interdependent Identity	Extremely difficult and painful	Establish separate lives that are always interconnected
Split Identity	Relief for twins	After separation maintain a distant relationship
Individual Identity	Difficult transition	After separation remain best and trusted friends

The use of fertility drugs in the 1980s increased the prevalence of twin births. Since then, substantial research has been done on parenting twins and twin development. Twin groups and educators began to emphasize individuality when talking to parents. The cuteness of twinship was less glamorized and idealized by parents. Parents, teachers, and pediatricians became aware that they needed to focus on developing unique personalities in twins and overcome the potential socialization and language difficulties that can develop if twins are always together and treated as a pair.

Today, the parents of twins are urged to continually reevaluate their child-rearing practices so that their twins have enough separate experiences. Currently, many experts have come forth to help parents reduce serious developmental problems for twins (Malmstrom & Poland, 1999). Some experts give strict advice on how to separate twins, as if there were one recipe or strategy that works for all twins of all ages. Parents can become obsessed with putting their twins into appropriate separation experiences or routines. But whether separation is appropriate in a certain situation depends on the twins' closeness and how they behave in relationships with other children and adults. For example, a mother with a great deal of self-confidence may be able to take her twins everywhere together and still treat them as individuals. But their father may be incapable of dealing with both children at the same time and leave one with Grandma or the baby-sitter for convenience, not because he is trying to develop individuality. Also, young twins who are capable of functioning individually but who have recently experienced a serious loss or setback may need each other's comfort.

No one would argue that this trend toward seeing twins as individuals and not as cute freaks of nature is dangerous. Obviously, twins deserve to be treated with respect rather than with circuslike attention. However, parents and other primary caregivers need to be attuned to what twins may need in different situations. Practicality is always an issue. Forcing separation between young twins may not foster individuality; rather, it may foster regression, such as clinging behavior, and inattention or distraction.

Composite View of Separation in Childhood

Beatrice and Maggie go to kindergarten. They love walking to school together every day with a set of fraternal boy-girl twins, Jennifer and Josh.

Maggie and Beatrice have a hard time concentrating without each other when they are placed in different classrooms. Beatrice leaves her classroom to talk to Maggie without asking the teacher if she can be excused. Maggie never asks permission to leave her chair and often wanders around the classroom, looking lost. The girls have to be together in kindergarten so they can concentrate on school tasks.

By first grade Maggie and Beatrice have grown up enough to be in separate classrooms, listen to their teachers, stay in their seats, and follow directions. They are both excellent at learning to read but dislike math concepts. Both girls are very sociable at recess and lunch. They play together and make new friends.

In second grade Mrs. Kramer, their mother, speaks to the girls' teacher, who encourages her to dress Maggie and Bea in different clothes so the other children at school can tell them apart more easily. Bea and Maggie at first resist this new idea because they enjoy looking alike and want to have exactly the same clothes. Gradually the girls adjust to dressing differently—their mother introduces individuality in dressing slowly. First, Mrs. Kramer buys the girls different shoes, then different pants and shirts, until months later Bea and Maggie wear completely different clothes at school. At home they still dress alike.

Jennifer and Josh, their twin friends, have not had the same problems separating from each other. Being different genders, they have never dressed alike, of course.

By the time Beatrice and Maggie are in the third grade, it is apparent to their teachers and family members that Maggie is the more socially outgoing twin. Beatrice is quieter and likes to play with only one friend at a time. She spends a great deal of time with Jennifer. Maggie has a group of girls with whom she likes to play at school. She is more active in sports and is more of a tomboy than her sister.

Maggie and Bea do all of their homework togther after school. They always seem to be able to achieve the same grades, which makes both girls happy. If one twin does better than the other, they both cry. Mrs. Kramer is just pleased whenever her girls are calm. No one in the family understands why both girls cry when only one of them is having trouble.

Today Bea and Maggie are joining the Brownies. They are excited that they get to wear the same outfit, small brown dresses, that all the girls in the troop wear. Both girls love dressing alike. Bea checks out how Maggie looks in her Brownie dress and vice versa. The dresses are a little tight because the girls have been sneaking too many cookies. Maggie runs off to play with the girls at the jungle gym, hoping to shed some pounds. Beatrice looks for Jennifer and they go play on the swings.

COMMON SEPARATION PROBLEMS OF TWINS IN THIS STUDY

The separation experiences of the adult twins with whom I spoke had some common denominators.

Sadness When the Twins Were First Separated

First, all the twins I interviewed had difficulty separating from their twin sibling when they were infants and toddlers. They would cry and cling to their mothers if they were apart from their twin for too long. The length of time twins could tolerate being apart depended on their age. Infants needed to be close to their twin as much as humanly possible. One-year-old twins could be in separate rooms and play happily, but briefly. As twins got older they learned to separate physically from each other for longer periods of time. By kindergarten most twins were in separate classrooms.

Withdrawal is another possible reaction of missing the twin in early childhood. The twins with whom I spoke did not report feeling withdrawn when they were not with their twin sibling. However, they thought that the experience of becoming isolated and withdrawn was possible.

The twins with whom I spoke were usually separated from each other in kindergarten. Parents and teachers were sensitive to these children's struggles about separation, and separation anxiety, although present, was not overwhelming. None of the twins were pressured to separate if it became apparent that they needed each other. Interestingly, some twins remembered getting out of their separate beds in the middle of the night in order to sleep with each other, well through early childhood.

School-Age Twins Were Able to Tolerate Separate Experiences

School-age twins were able to tolerate not being in class with their sister or brother, although they needed to see each other outside the classroom. Some twins went to diffferent schools without being overly stressed or regressed. School-age twins preferred to share interests, insights, friends, and clothes. Most managed to achieve at a similar pace. When twins were not performing similarly, one twin was held behind so the other could catch up. Twins who had been directly encouraged to express their individuality were motivated to seek out separate friends and separate interests earlier than twins who had not received this type of encouragement.

Adolescents Sought Out Separate Friends

By early adolescence all of the twins with whom I spoke were distinctly interested in having separate friends from their twin. Often, a twin took on a distinct persona as the wild twin or the goody-goody twin to establish a different lifestyle and different friends. In adolescence twins dealt with separation issues related to a greater need for independence by checking in with their sister or brother on a daily basis if possible. Dating seemed to be a strong motivator of independent behavior for twins. Usually the boyfriend or girl-friend relationship was strong enough to encourage twins to live more separate lives.

Early Marriage Was Common

Early marriages were not uncommon for the twins in this study. Eighty percent of them married in their 20s. Marriage, then having children of their own, created separate and distinctive worlds for twins, who still kept in close contact with their twin sibling if possible. The spouse and children replaced the companionship of the twin. Twins who did not marry got involved in serious relationships and careers to replace the intensity of twinship.

Although early marriage is also common for non-twins as a way of establishing separateness and distinctiveness from the family of origin, the quality of the search for identity in a relationship with another person is very different for twins than for non-twins. I have worked professionally with many young men and women in psychotherapy who use marriage to grow up and away. These single-born people seem less concerned with the quality of their attachment to their new husband or new wife than the twins who participated in my research project.

Problems Communicating with Others

All the twins I interviewed had trouble communicating their feelings and ideas with their parents and other people. They preferred to communicate with their attentive co-twin, who seemed to have an immediate and deep understanding of their problems. In every twinship, both twins reported that they did not even have to ask for help from their sister or brother—it was just available. Most twins could read each other's minds at some time in their lives.

Besides their co-twin, finding someone to solve problems and help out quickly was impossible to find in childhood or even in adolescence. Twins strongly missed and longed for the deep understanding they found in their twinship.

Missing the Identity of Being a Twin

All the twins in this study were aware that they missed being a twin when they were physically separated because of illness or because they attended separate summer camps. This unexpected experience of being with other people, without their twin, was eerie for them. They felt less special as well as strange when they realized that they had to relate to other people as a non-twin. Most twins discussed this problem with each other and developed strategies to deal with the non-twin world. For example, twin boys were sent to separate camps during the summer after completing sixth grade. They discussed with each other how to talk, act, and dress so they would feel accepted.

Looking for Relationship Replacements for the Twin

Separating from a twin in adolescence meant finding a close relationship to replace the void left by the twin sibling. All of the twins with whom I spoke sought out new relationships through dating, sports, and academic or artistic endeavors. Most interestingly, none of the twins chose to be alone and pursue solitary interests or careers. Rather, they sought out people-oriented experiences and long-term friendships or marriages.

Sharing

The participants in this study enjoyed sharing thoughts, feelings, and experiences with each other. Twinship is a highly open-ended collaborative experience.

Competition

As young children, competition was an issue for all the twin pairs. They remember being compared and contrasted with each other scholastically, physically, and socially. Competing with each other and enduring comparisons with their twin sibling were naturally accepted as a part of twinship. As twins became more separate, they gradually began to resent comparisons that others made about them. Twins consolidated their own identities in late adolescence and rebelled against being measured against each other.

THE IMPACT OF TRAUMATIC STRESS ON SEPARATION ISSUES

Traumatic stress in early childhood and adolescence affected how twins related to separating from their parents and from each other. The adult twins with whom I spoke experienced the following traumatic events: World War II, immigration, sexual abuse, divorce or other divisive family conflicts, and being raised by alcoholic parents.

Twins had opposing reactions to these stressful situations. The twins who experienced serious external traumas became closer and used each other to cope with terrifying events. The twins who faced internal pressures within their family, such as child and sexual abuse, alcoholism, or divorce, seemed to turn away from each other as older adolescents. They looked outside of their family structure for emotional support and decidedly did not cling to each other as a coping strategy. These twins were determined to find new support systems outside of their twinship.

External Stressors

The following examples illustrate how twins used each other in the face of overwhelming trauma. Once again, names and places have been changed to protect the privacy of the adults in this study.

Natalie and Veronica, identical twins, were born in Eastern Europe at the beginning of World War II. Their parents were wealthy Jews with many contacts through their business dealings. When the Germans invaded their hometown, the family was forced to split up. Veronica and Natalie were sent to live with a Christian family and were subsequently treated as Christians. Their parents hid underground during the German occupation.

When World War II was over, Natalie and Veronica were reunited with their parents. The family lived in three European countries before finally emigrating to the United States. These twins were adolescents when their parents established a new, permanent home. Many adjustments and stresses were endured as the girls integrated into American culture after spending their childhoods as Europeans. Together, Natalie and Veronica learned English and how to cope with being American teenagers.

Memories of the terror of war in Eastern Europe and the family's long journey to safety in America left indelible mental scars. The non-verbal and verbal sharing of these painful memories brought Natalie and Veronica closer. They remember their vivid fear when the German invasion took place. As five-year-old twins, they had experienced unspeakable terror that they believed that others could not possibly understand. Veronica and Natalie's already close identification with each other was intensified. Their bond with each other developed deeper roots because of the traumatic stress of their childhood and the subsequent adjustments of adolescence.

Natalie and Veronica had been treated by their mother and father as individuals with distinctive personalities. Because of their sense of separateness they were able to part from each other as adolescents. They each married and had their own families and careers, but emotionally Veronica and Natalie have always felt closer to each other than to anyone else in their lives. I believe they stayed so close because of the external traumas they experienced.

Ida and Eleanor, also identical twins, were born in a concentration camp and separated from their mother and father in early infancy. They were raised in the concentration camp by friends of the family after their parents were killed. Ida and Eleanor gradually made their way to England after the war with their adoptive parents. They report clinging to each other throughout their early childhood. Although they lost their parents, Eleanor and Ida's immigration to the United States appears to have been an easier transition than what Natalie and Veronica experienced. Acculturation in California was less stressful because they spoke English and had not been raised as Europeans. However, these twins remained "joined at the hip" emotionally. Their unit identity, caused by the lack of parenting they received in the concentration camp and the horrors of wartime experience, intensified their relationship. The roots of Eleanor and Ida's twinship were enmeshed and intertwined to such an extent that they were never able to separate from each other. They slept in the same bed through adolescence. Although they each dated, they never married or developed separate interests and careers. Their childhood traumas and their twinship created a bond that was rigid and fixed; their identities were coalesced. Ida and Eleanor cannot live without each other.

Eileen and Jean were born in a British colony to wealthy and educated parents. They remember clearly that their parents could tell them apart as soon as they were home from the hospital. Eileen, a social worker, believes that their early individuality was related to the differences in their genetic endowment, because they are fraternal twins. Jean, a teacher, believes their mother and father made serious efforts to separate and relate to their twin children. Although Jean and Eileen don't agree on how individual differences were precisely established between them, they agree that they were treated as individual members of a twin pair. Eileen said, "We don't look alike at all but we wanted to believe that we thought alike." They remember how special they felt about being twins. Their family experienced feelings of being left out and was even jealous of their close relationship. Jean and Eileen cherished and idealized their twinship.

Eileen and Jean immigrated to different countries for political reasons and to gain citizenship. They both held on to the fantasy that they would be "together once again in the same country." Eileen told me that it took her more than 10 years to overcome the painful loss of not being close to her sister. She realizes that she held on to this fantasy because the pain of losing physical contact with her sister was extremely intense.

The fantasy of coming into close physical proximity was perpetuated by the pain of a long-distance separation. Remember that early in Eileen and Jean's lives they felt special because they were twins. They held on to their sense of being special in order to cope with the enormous and long-standing stress of moving to new and separate continents. Fortunately, Jean and Eileen had their

own sense of themselves as individuals as well as twins. Although they idealized their closeness, they were able to function on their own. They married
and pursued their own careers. Later in life, as new emotional stresses arose,
Jean and Eileen dealt with the pain of physical separation more realistically.
They were eventually able to give up their idealized sense of their twinship
and develop a realistic view of each other.

Internal Stressors

   Internal family stress had the opposite effect on the bond between twins and
on the twins' capacity to live separate lives and hold on to their early cherished
closeness. In homes where young twins experienced serious emotional neglect,
sexual abuse, or a bitter conflicted divorce that included mental suffering, separation between the pairs was dramatic and long-standing.
   The following twin pairs had strong reactions to the stress of internal family
conflicts. Their life experiences reflect how family conflicts can create distance
between twins.
   Ann and Arlene, fraternal twins, were born and raised in Southern California. Their parents had not planned on having more children, so when Ann and
Arlene were born, both mother and father felt overwhelmed and burdened.
Unfortunately, their mother could not deal with the stress of raising twins. She
started drinking as a way to numb her anger at her twin children and the
burden of parenting them. Ann recalls that her mother was mean, depressed,
weak, and ineffectual. The twin girls were not treated as individuals, but rather,
as one unit. Any distinctions that were made between the twins were based on
decisions between the two girls. Parenting was not available to establish individuality.
   As they grew up, their mother fell more heavily into drinking. Ann recalls
the relief she felt when she came home from school to find her mother playing
solitaire and drinking, instead of being mean and critical of her and her sister.
Their father, who was in total denial of his wife's alcohol abuse, child abuse,
and neglect, would come home only for dinner. There was no attempt to deal
with the family problems that grew out of the mother's alcoholism. Ann and
Arlene did all the cooking, dishwashing, laundry, and other household chores.
Their mother died of cirrhosis of the liver when the twins were 16 years old.
Their father still denied his wife's alcoholic behavior and the scars the children
had suffered because of her abuse.
   Ann and Arlene had emotional difficulties separating from each other in late
adolescence. They shared an interdependent identity: Ann was the responsible
parental twin and Arlene was the social, outgoing, and impulsive twin. The
girls sought out psychotherapy in their early 20s to deal with the problems of
missing each other. Psychotherapy was unsuccessful in dealing with Arlene's
shame about her impulsivity or with Ann's inability to accept or contain her
sister's problems.

Arlene moved to Chicago after marrying a stockbroker. She lived a jet-set life for six months without her sister. When her husband's stock portfolio was hurt by bad business dealings, their marriage began to fall apart. Arlene became very depressed and sought out a psychiatrist. Even though Ann lived 3,000 miles from her twin sister, they spoke on the phone nightly. Ann tried to help Arlene be more hopeful, and she planned to visit in a few weeks. Before she made it, Arlene committed suicide. When Ann was told by Arlene's husband that her sister had asphyxiated herself in the garage, her world stopped. "Arlene didn't mean to kill herself," she said. "She didn't think suicide was permanent." Arlene's suicide was a direct result of her being separated from her twin, growing up in an alcoholic household, and her impulsive personality.

Another example of childhood abuse and mental suffering that created anger and early separation between twins was reported by Mary and Melinda. These identical twins were welcomed into an educated and seemingly principled religious family. Their mother was delighted to have twins even though she was overwhelmed by their care. Her husband was not delighted with his twin daughters, who seemed to demand so much attention and caused so many problems in the home. He actually disliked Melinda for reasons no one in the nuclear or extended family could explain. The father picked on Melinda and favored Mary, and their brother took Dad's lead. Both twins suffered from the erratic behavior and anger of their brother and father, and from their mother's passivity in setting limits for her husband and son. Melinda remembers being sexually molested by her father and brother, but Mary reports no memory of actual moments when her sister's sexual privacy was invaded. Even though the facts of sexual abuse remembered differently by these twins are unverifiable, emotional reality reflects the abuse (Schave, 1994).

Mary and Melinda were relieved to separate from their family when they left home for college. They roomed together for one semester and continued to feel disappointed or burdened by each other. They realized that they were happier apart as they enjoyed meeting new people and developing separate interests. As Melinda and Mary entered their 20s, they both wanted to forget about their twinship. Early sexual abuse created a deep schism between these twins, who preferred not to have contact with each other.

Cynthia and Arnold, fraternal twins, were born into a poor Catholic family. Their parents were highly intelligent people, but they were unable to support their twins. These children had to wear the same clothes every day and did not have enough to eat. Arnold had difficulty concentrating in school, so he was placed in a special classroom for children with Attention Deficit Disorder. Cynthia had no learning problems and was much better adjusted than her brother, but she constantly worried about Arnold's capacity to make friends. Their parents were unable to get psychological help for Arnold. Another disaster soon besieged the family when their mother received a diagnosis of terminal cancer.

After their mother's death, Cynthia and Arnold's life became more emotionally unstable, although their father made some good business transactions that allowed for financial security. There was enough money to send Cynthia to college, whereas Arnold, who had a poor academic record, went to work in his father's business. Without the presence of their mother, Cynthia and Arnold fought over their father's decision to send only one child to college. Arnold later paid for his own college education. A rift between these twins started, and they grew more distant as the years went by. Cynthia became a social worker and married. Arnold became an extremely wealthy businessman who had many unhappy marriages. The twins were unable to turn to each other for emotional support for more than 25 years.

Dede and Diana are identical twins who were raised by a psychologically minded mother, who made every effort to encourage what was unique in each of her children. At the time of their birth the family was very prosperous and Dede and Diana received a great deal of attention and love. Their early childhood was described as idyllic. Unfortunately, the wealth and financial stability of the family was slowly eroded by their father's mental illness. Although their insightful and empathetic mother was determined to protect them from their father's rage, her efforts were not successful. Diana and Dede had become afraid of their father by the time their mother finally filed for divorce. Dede went to live with her best friend and Diana lived with her mother. These twins attended the same colleges, but their lives took separate paths. Dede went on to medical school and became a doctor, and Diana enjoys an equestrian lifestyle.

TYPICAL PATTERNS OF SEPARATION IN
EARLY ADOLESCENCE

Twins who lived through early adolescence without the pressures of internal and external traumatic events reacted to separation from their twin in a more developmentally typical manner (Schave & Schave, 1989). As is typical of adolescents, rebellion against childhood rules was apparent. Specific for twins was the rebellion and reaction to dressing alike and to the ever-present question, "Are you twins?" In addition, twins sought out more separate and distinct friendships. They began to date members of the opposite sex and to establish distinctive academic or career interests. Twins still continued to be each other's special counsel on all important decisions.

The following examples are illustrative of early adolescent twins:

Cathy and Carol, identical twins with an interdependent identity bond, were very close in childhood. They always dressed alike and shared friends and interests. In early adolescence they finally chose to dress differently. Carol was more offbeat in style, whereas Cathy was conservative. They began dating different types of young men.

Cindy and Debbie, identical twins with a split identity, were very concerned about looking exactly alike when they were children. As early adolescents they began to dress in different outfits, which they liked to trade. Both girls began to suffer from an eating disorder. Although they dressed differently, they were obsessed about being exactly the same size and weight.

Liz and Lonnie were constant playmates in childhood. Although they did not dress alike and had different friends, they were clearly identifiable as twins. In junior high school they took on different personas. Liz, who had learning disabilities and had difficulty in school, colored her hair red and pink and became a punk rocker. Lonnie, who was a good student, followed a more preppie look and became a cheerleader.

Early adolescent separation was difficult for all of the adult twins with whom I spoke. Some of these twins successfully became distinctive personalities, whereas others remained intertwined in each other's lives. Parental attachment, as well as internal and external life stressors, directly affected the degree and quality of each early separation experience.

3

The Identity Dilemma

A CONCEPTUALIZATION OF IDENTITY

Identity is a theoretical or psychological construct that has long fascinated philosophers, writers, poets, psychologists, and psychoanalysts. What constitutes identity or personality depends on whom you are referring to or speaking with. Many anthropologists and psychoanalytical theorists believe that your identity can be traced back to your direct ancestors because of the strong influence of family values and overall genetic endowments (Socarides & Stolorow, 1984–85). Other contemporary psychoanalysts, though, focus on the parent-child interaction as the driving force behind personality (Basch, 1982; Beebe & Lachman, 1988). Behavioral theory suggests that our identity is determined by our parents and our own responses, which have been learned from childhood experiences (Bell, 1977; Chess & Thomas, 1963). Existential philosophies maintain that the individual is responsible for his or her own actions or choices, rejecting the idea that there is a greater underlying meaning to life than the present moment. Identity is transient. Last, developmental theorists say the self evolves from affective interactions with parents and significant others (Demos, 1982; Cotton, 1985; Stern, 1985).

I have chosen to conceptualize identity as comprising all of the above theoretical components. Simply stated, our identity/personality is derived from our distant past, our childhood past, our present relationships, and our hopes for the future. When interviewing the twins in this study, I was concerned with their past cultural backgrounds, their families' social and economic status, the social and educational values they were raised with, their genetic endowment, the quality of parenting they received, the external stressors they had to confront, and whether they were passive or active determinants of their own well-being. Maintaining a positive sense of self-esteem seemed to be a function of identity that promoted adaptive and coping strategies. The self-concept and self-esteem that the interviewees were able to maintain throughout their life experiences were significant, because the capacity to feel hopeful and self-confident was a crucial determinant of overall well-being.

The following interview protocol was used to obtain a sense of the development of identity in the twins who participated in this study. Interviews were conducted with each member of the twin pair, separately, on the phone or in person. Answers between twins in a pair were not shared. Material outside of the interview questions that came up and was determined to be pertinent to identity was included in the findings.

- What is your earliest memory of being a twin?
- How would you describe your parents' attitude about having twins?
- What was the family's financial and social situation at the time of your birth?
- Did you have siblings and how did they feel about having twins?
- How did your parents see you as different than your twin?
- When were you first separated from your twin?
- What was it like for you to separate from your twin?
- What is your earliest memory of not being with your twin?
- Did you attend school together?
- When do you think you started to want to be more distinctive from your twin?
- Did you dress alike until you felt the need to be seen as an individual?
- What was it like to have other children know you were a twin?
- How would you describe the differences between you and your twin?
- How did your parents deal with issues of competition?
- How did your relationship with your twin change over time?
- Do you feel that you had or still have a distinct twin identity?
- Did you need to re-create your twinship with other very close relationships in your life?
- Was it hard for you to develop adult relationships outside of the twinship?
- Did you ever feel that significant others could not understand what it was like for you to be a twin?
- How did your children deal with you being a twin?
- Did you ever feel lonely in non-twinlike relationships?
- What kinds of life experiences brought you closer to your twin?
- What life experiences created differences and distance between you and your twin?
- How would you describe your present relationship with your twin?
- Was the bond you share or shared with your twin the most influential in your life? If not, why not, and what was more important?
- How would you compare your twinship to the parent-child bonding experience?
- Do you think the bond with your twin is different than a bond with a sibling? Please explain.
- What was the most positive part of being a twin?
- What was the most difficult part of growing up as a twin?

The following topics were added to the interview because of input from the participants:

- Did you ever wish that you were not a twin?
- How did your family and your twin relate to your sexual identity, i.e., homosexuality or heterosexuality?
- Have you ever had to deal with the possible loss/death of your twin?
- Have you ever been treated in psychotherapy?

The research design of this project was grounded in the theory of qualitative injury, or case study approach (Cresswell, 1996).

IDENTITY DIFFERENCES IN TWINS

Twins have distinctive issues forming their identities compared with single children because twins share the ultimate closeness. They share their mother's womb, their parents, possessions, and early memories. They also have a public image as a twin pair, which is highly visible and attracts much curiosity and attention. In terms of public personas, twins may be too close for comfort.

The private relationship twins share is highly competitive. They measure themselves against each other for many reasons. First, all twins have a narcissistic investment in each other; that is, they think their twin is a direct reflection of who they are. This is, of course, understandable, since twins are often treated as a unit or pair by parents and twin onlookers. More important, very early in their lives twins pay attention to and respond to their sibling's feelings, thoughts, and appearance, because of the physical and emotional closeness they share. Because the co-twin is one's close friend and constant companion, concern for one's twin is normal, given the investment that twins have in each other's well-being.

This investment in twinship, though, can lead to problems as twins grow up and desire, or need, to be on their own. Because they become used to experiencing everything together, twins do not learn how to perform simple tasks alone. They "check in" with each other all the time for mundane reasons, such as deciding which doughnut is the best of the dozen. Having each other gives them a lead on which choice to make—red jelly or lemon? Twins delight in making decisions together, but what happens when the other twin is not there to help? A twin will feel more confused, even out of sorts, than a single child would. The disappointment is palpable.

For twins who are used to checking with each other for input, unforeseen complications caused by distraction or foolhardiness are a real hazard. Twins playing with matches are definitely double trouble, as are twins with poisonous household chemicals. Unfortunately, twins can jointly make decisions that are dangerous and self-destructive.

Later on in life, choices have to be made without the input of a twin sister or brother, leading to trouble for the twin who lacks the judgment and experience to make the decision alone. This was a common problem for twins who married early and were unprepared to meet the demands of a relationship so different than twinship.

Another fascinating aspect of twin identity is the question of dominance. Is there really a dominant and non-dominant twin, as suggested by many twin researchers? (Burlingham, 1952; Koch, 1966; Leonard, 1961; Schave, 1982). The twins who participated in this study reported that dominance issues, which included power balances between the pair, did exist and varied depending on the situation and time in their lives. For example, one twin might take a dominant role in the kindergarten classroom and the other twin might be dominant at home. With adult twins, one might be dominant financially, whereas the other is dominant as a mother figure or surrogate parent.

Clearly, twins develop idiosyncratic identity problems because of the almost all-consuming presence of the twin sibling in infancy, early childhood, and later childhood. It would be an oversimplification to say that twins lack experience acting on their own, and that this creates problems with self-expression and self-confidence. Rather, it makes more sense to say that twins have a well-developed concept of who they are because of the continual feedback they receive from their co-twin and from significant other and twin onlookers. However, being a twin in a non-twin world presents distinct challenges, disappointments, and opportunities because of the differences a twin experiences in developing his or her sense of self.

Emergence of Separate Identity Issues in Adolescence

In childhood, identity issues are defined by the individual attention each twin needs, and the individual attention he receives. As stated in Chapters 1 and 2, individual attention in childhood is related to the quality of parenting. The bond that twins share serves to define who a twin is very distinctly.

Adolescence is a time when there is a stronger focus on differences between twins. The period of adolescence is a developmental stage that entails an intense search for a unique sense of self (Schave & Schave, 1989). Sexuality is awakened and used at first to seek out new relationships with the opposite sex, or in some instances the same sex. Cognitive capacity, including the capacity for abstract thinking, allows adolescent twins to look at themselves and their family from a different perspective (Flavell, 1977; Piaget, 1950).

During the adolescent years, a twin begins to move away from her twin sibling and define herself as a separate person, without her sister. Friendships with the opposite sex take on new meanings because they are not shared. Academic and career options allow for different choices among the pair that reflect each person's unique strengths and talents.

Composite View of Adolescence

Imagine the following scenario, a composite of the twin profiles of this study. Beatrice and Maggie, the inseparable T-1 and T-2, are teenagers. They have finally decided to dress differently all the time, really differently, not just in different colors. Their mother has spent countless hours shopping with them, and Beatrice and Maggie have searched on their own for perfect outfits in high school and their hoped-for party lives. Shopping for the twins is a fun but serious challenge. They are very interested in how many more outfits they can have if each girl has different clothes. The mathematical computations of possibilities are mind-boggling and more interesting to the girls than algebra.

Maggie and Beatrice are excellent students with high grades and the determination to succeed in school and go on to college. They have always measured their achievements and accomplishments against each other. If Beatrice has problems in math, Maggie helps her, and when Maggie has difficulties in Hebrew and French, Beatrice comes to her aid. The girls have never had a tutor because tutoring is built into the relationship.

Beatrice is beginning to show interest in the opposite sex. She talks to Maggie about whom she is interested in, and Maggie advises her on the best approach to landing a lunch date. Maggie is more of a tomboy and a socialite who wants to join a girls' club. Beatrice is not interested in being a club girl. When Maggie is rejected from the girls' club, having Beatrice cushions the blow. They still have many of the same friends and their grades are similar, but they are interested in different boyfriends.

A new era in Beatrice and Maggie's twin counseling emerges. They have been each other's adviser in school, home, and clothing matters for an entire lifetime, but dating adds a new twist. Fortunately, they don't want to share their boyfriends. They may want to double-date once in a while, but the choice of a romantic partner is something they cannot agree on. Beatrice and Maggie try to minimize their dislike for each other's boyfriends, but for the rest of their lives this will be a struggle. In spite of different tastes in men, they go to the prom as double dates and they choose to go to the same college.

Away from home at college Maggie and Beatrice begin to have more and more individual experiences. Their separate identities are becoming apparent. They don't need to share all of their coordinating clothes, but if it works out that they can, they feel delighted and lucky. Beatrice starts studying art seriously and Maggie becomes interested in history. New friends are added and new academic interests help establish their own separate lives. They still are best friend and trusted counsel to each other. Often they generously and thoughtfully give each other the space to make their own decisions. Sometimes they are critical of each other's choices. When there is a disagreement, whether it is about careers, friends, or travel plans, they talk about it or fight it out. There's a lot of open communication between Beatrice and Maggie.

COMMON IDENTITY STRUGGLES OF TWINS IN THIS STUDY

Twins Were Measured Against Each Other

All of the twins I interviewed believed that part of their identity or personality was related to the reality that they were continually measured against each other while growing up. Twins internalized the comparisons others made between them and always compared themselves with each other. This focus on what was similar about their experiences and what was different made them very aware, almost self-conscious, of the choices they made. In many situations twins' identities, whether as a pair or as an individual, was overdetermined because of the amount of attention it received.

Competition Was an Integral and Acceptable Part of Their Identity

The twins with whom I spoke thought competition was a strong motivator in their capacity to function outside of their twin relationship. In other words, twins were able to use the positive aspects of competing with their twin siblings in school, personal interests, and careers. They did not think that having to be evaluated continually threatened their self-esteem. Rather, the competitiveness of their childhood was a jump start for other competitive situations they had to deal with while growing up. The twins I interviewed enjoy competition and take it seriously. They are not easily overwhelmed by the stress of competitive situations because they have more than adequate coping strategies to deal with such evaluations.

Establishing Relationships Outside of the Twinship Was Problematic

The companionship and intensity of the twinship created obstacles for twins when they wanted to form different relationships. Adolescent and adult twins had difficulty understanding what constituted appropriate expectations for new relationships. Twins consciously and unconsciously regressed into thinking that they could expect the same intensity with new people in their lives as they had with their twin sibling. A twin's expectations for intensity and intimacy with others defined his personality struggles in adolescence and through midlife.

Early Marriage Was Extremely Common

Eighty percent of the twins I spoke with married for the first time in their early 20s. They saw marriage as a comfortable way to define themselves outside of being a twin. Most twins had children from these marriages with whom they formed deep attachments. Although it is difficult to compare this sample of twins with an imaginary sample of single people because of the variation in ages and other demographics, speculatively it seems that twins are more likely to marry at an early age compared with non-twins.

Twins Communicated About Marriage and Career Choices

All of the twins in this study had long, deep conversations with each other about the different paths they would take in their lives. Twins were open with each other about strengths and weaknesses in their decisions. They were not afraid to hurt each other's feelings when actual choices were being made. In sum, each twin was a counselor for the other in establishing the outward character of her identity.

Moving Away from the Closeness of Twinship Was Perceived as Normal

Each of the twins I interviewed wanted to have some separate space from their brother or sister. A twin did not feel guilty leaving her role of childhood look-alike to establish a separate and distinct identity. In fact, she was her sister's advocate in her search for a distinctive identity, and her twin was hers.

UNIQUE IDENTITY STRUGGLES OF TWINS

The specific pattern of twinship that twins shared created some unique identity struggles. Twins with a unit identity or interdependent identity did not successfully separate from each other. When they attempted to separate and form a new identity, they found that their bond was too deeply rooted and intertwined. Split identity twins developed separate lives, but each sibling held onto his childhood identity as a good or bad person. Individual identity twins successfully separated from each other after adolescence, and they remained trusted friends.

Unit Identity

Eleanor and Ida—Entwined Lives

Ida and Eleanor, who were born in a German concentration camp, share an enmeshed bond. They lived in England as young children and traveled to the United States with their adoptive parents, eventually settling in California. Ida and Eleanor both completed college and started pursuing different careers, but they were so reliant upon each other that they were unable to separate for longer than was absolutely necessary. They attempted to form attachments with other people but were unable to maintain them because of the overwhelming intensity of their own bond. Eleanor and Ida worked in related fields and

relied upon each other on a daily basis. They did not develop a complete separate identity from each other—only together were they able to function in the
world.

Interdependent Identity

Ann and Arlene—Forever Together

Ann and Arlene shared an interdependent identity because of a lack of parenting and long-term abuse from an alcoholic mother. As they grew up, they
went their separate ways and began to develop distinct personalities. Ann was
very shy and serious, whereas Arlene was social and impulsive. Unfortunately,
Arlene, the seemingly lighthearted, fun-loving twin, committed suicide in her
mid-20s because she was overwhelmed by the disintegration of her marriage
and without her sister was unable to make rational decisions. Ann believes that
Arlene did not mean to take such a drastic, final measure, but that her sister
needed her attention, strength, and hope for the future to overcome her despair.
Ann was devastated by the loss of her sister. It took her 10 years to feel like
the "hole in her chest" had mended.

Her recovery from this tragedy and enormous loss involved establishing her
own identity as an individual. Ann has four children whom she loves and to
whom she gives her heart. After 10 years of mourning she also entered psychotherapy. This therapeutic alliance helped her leave her husband and begin
a career in financial management. Ann enjoyed getting feedback as an adult
and worked very hard to give her children everything they needed. Unlike her
mother, Ann is devoted and attentive to her children. Still, she has never felt
comfortable forming deep friendships—her career and children are the focus
of her identity.

Ann believes her capacity to live on after her sister's death is directly related
to raising her children and to understanding what the loss of her sister means
to her. Her struggles with identity are unique.

Serena and Candy—Halves of a Whole

Serena and Candy, who share an interdependent identity, were born in the
South. Their maternal grandmother was a twin, as was their mother. They
remember their mother and father were overwhelmed and struggling, and they
agreed, "It was enough that they just fed us." Candy and Serena were always
treated as if they were one person. Serena states, "We are fraternal twins who
look very much alike," Serena said. "We were lumped together a lot."

Serena and Candy both recall that their mother was mean, hateful, and
judgmental. The girls received very little emotional support from either parent.
What they remember about receiving attention as children is that they were
both punished for making trouble even if only one of them had caused the

problem. Positive attention was not readily available, and the girls turned to each other for love and affection.

Candy and Serena recollect their childhood as being very close. Their parents could easily distinguish between them because they parted their hair differently, but otherwise they were not treated as different individuals. Their mother did place them in separate classrooms starting in kindergarten, because she thought it would help them become more individualized. This was very hard for them, and Candy and Serena spent recess and after-school time together until high school.

Serena and Candy dressed alike until seventh grade. They had the same friends, attended music and dance lessons together, and wrote for the school yearbook together. In adolescence they established a difference between themselves, like other twins in this study, by dating dissimilar types of boys. Their first arguments focused on how boys they were dating treated them. Each girl thought her sister was being mistreated by her boyfriend.

Candy and Serena attended the same college and both studied interior design. Candy recalls that Serena became more interested in materialistic, socially connected men in college. Serena remembers that Candy became more interested in men with whom she could have fun. Serena became the serious twin and Candy the lighthearted twin. In spite of the development of personality differences by late adolescence, these girls remained very close to each other in young adulthood. They needed each other to make decisions. Together they felt complete, and it seemed as though they were making better life choices when they consulted with each other.

Candy and Serena both disagreed about each other's decision to marry, but nonetheless accepted their twin's choice. Candy recalls wanting her own wedding dress because she thought Serena's was too fancy. They married within several months of each other and immediately started their families. Candy and Serena continued to rely on each other for advice and emotional support as they began separate lives. They spoke on a weekly basis, their children played with one another, and they visited each other as frequently as possible. The reality of children and their economic needs forced them to tolerate each other's husband, but it was not easy.

Serena and Candy had established their own identities by the time they married, but they continued to rely on each other to a much greater extent than twins with a split identity or an individual identity. Of the 30 sets of twins I interviewed, four pairs shared an interdependent identity. I have chosen to write about Ann and Arlene and Candy and Serena because they are different but excellent examples of the interdependent identity twin bond. Although these twins established separate identities, their reliance on each other was extremely tenacious. They lived intertwined lives—their primary connection was to their twin sibling. Husbands and parents were much less significant relationships, but they formed strong attachments with their children.

Split Identity

Emily and Deena—An Unresolved Twinship

Emily and Deena were the youngest children in a family of seven. Their parents were Eastern European immigrants who were delighted to have twins. However, dealing with both twins was difficult for this old-world family, so Deena and Emily were treated as a unit. Early in their lives, each twin recalls, Deena was the bossy one who was labeled the good girl and Emily was continually the troublemaker.

Emily and Deena were child entertainers—their earliest memory is of dancing and singing on stage at their parents' country hotel. The twins loved performing together throughout their childhood. Their parents were proud to have their children on stage, and it kept the girls out of trouble. Emily and Deena otherwise tended to squabble if left unsupervised.

In spite of their fighting, Deena and Emily presented themselves to the outside world as happy "look-alike" twins, dressing alike until they attended college. They remember being very competitive with each other. Emily thinks there was more pressure on her to do well in school because people were aware that she was part of a twin pair. Whereas Emily felt pressured to be like Deena, Deena felt awkward and ashamed of her sister. Their relationship was complicated and conflicted.

Both girls longed for separate attention from their parents and teachers because they were not treated as individuals. Indeed, they tired of the attention they received as twins. At age eight, Emily recalls being happy that she was in the hospital alone without her sister because she got so much individual attention. Emily and Deena were not encouraged to go to college or have a career; their parents expected them to marry and help with the family business.

As with the other twins I interviewed, Deena and Emily met and married very different types of men. Emily always thought Deena had married into a higher status than she had. Deena was more financially secure than Emily, who was by no means poor. Emily's husband allowed her to pursue her dreams. Each woman had three children, but unlike many of the other twins with whom I spoke, Emily's children and Deena's children were not close to one another. Rather, their children and husbands supported the good and bad identities that Deena and Emily had taken on. Deena thought Emily had a troublesome family, and Emily thought Deena had an all-too-perfect family.

Deena and Emily's love-hate relationship was, and still is, based on dissatisfaction with each other and a longing for a better sense of connectedness. Their identities as twins and as separate people are in continual conflict. Each of these women is strong and competent on her own; each is self-aware and self-reflective. And each has spent her lifetime trying to resolve their relationship.

Mary and Melinda—Archenemies

Mary and Melinda were welcomed into their family and, like Deena and Emily, shared a polar opposite bond. They were high achievers, both straight-A students, and they competed with each other mercilessly, believing that they needed to be as much alike as possible. Mary was always on top and Melinda was always one step below. Even though these twins were bright, they never considered how ridiculous this game was until they were in late adolescence.

Competition was and still is a strong element of their identity. Fortunately, these girls did not compete for boyfriends; they were interested in different young men in high school. Melinda became more popular than Mary, which was not a plus in their competitive relationship because Mary was always supposed to be the best. Mary could never admit that she was jealous of Melinda, and Melinda's popularity was characterized as silly by her family.

College brought more distance between them as Mary and Melinda went their separate ways. Although they enjoyed the attention of being twins, which reminded them they were special, Mary and Melinda fought with each other over so many issues that it was best for them to spend as much time apart as possible. They studied different subjects in college and made very different friends. They did continue to share clothes whenever they saw each other.

Mary and Melinda married within 10 days of each other and shared a wedding dress. But Mary did not attend Melinda's wedding, and Melinda and her parents accepted this as normal or typical. Melinda had children right after marriage, and Mary was jealous that she was not the leader in this competition. Five years later Mary had her own children. Their families are not close—Mary and Melinda live in different states and pursue very different careers. They have had a turbulent adult relationship.

Both twin pairs, Emily and Deena and Mary and Melinda, share a bond that is very conflicted because they have been unconsciously and consciously identified as good and bad twins by their parents. Preferential treatment most likely begins unconsciously and then becomes a conscious interaction in the family. Split identity twins are content with their twinship as youngsters and in adolescence. They gain strength from the competitiveness that they perpetuate with each other. But they do not develop the closeness that other twins in this study share. Indeed, they seem to really dislike each other, but are afraid to accept their strong negative feelings of anger and disappointment and their shameful feelings. Emily summarized the issue poignantly: "I am afraid of my bad thoughts about being a twin," and added, "Twinship is a curse." Melinda feels that "being a twin made me a stronger person. The burden of my sister's problems do not weigh on me as they used to." Mary disagrees—she feels that being a twin made her special. Mary and Melinda can separate themselves from the burdens of being a twin.

Individual Identity

Peter and Raymond—Trusted Friends

Peter and Raymond, fraternal twins, were born into a family that was enthusiastic about having twins. These parents believed that it was easier to have two children at once. Both parents could tell their boys apart. Peter said, "We were never confused," and "my brother was more serious." "I was better with people," said Raymond, "Mother could tell us apart in a second. She treated us equally. She did not have a favorite son."

Peter and Raymond remember that they dressed alike until third grade and shared everything as young children. Activities included modeling and television commercials, which each twin remembers fondly.

Raymond and Peter developed an intense closeness as well as individual distinctiveness. Their parents separated them in kindergarten. By third grade they started to have their own friends and to develop different intellectual interests as well as different after-school interests. They recall having small fights growing up but gravitating toward each other in social situations.

As these twins grew into adolescence, they had each begun to develop a great deal of independence from each other. Although they attended the same high school and stayed in the same social groups, they went to different colleges and pursued different professions. Peter and Raymond married within two years of each other. They have remained very close, yet their lives are distinct.

Raymond and Peter see the closeness they shared as crucial to the development of their identities. They appear grateful that they have each other to provide emotional support. In addition, Peter and Raymond seem quite content in their separate lives. Although their wives do not get along with each other as well as they would like, they are able to tolerate this disharmony—they do not need to agree on everything.

Dorothy and Denise—Best of Buddies

Dorothy and Denise, red-haired identical twins, were born to well-to-do parents who were happy to have twins and "never made a big deal about us being twins." Their mother and father took parenting seriously and were psychologically minded enough to treat their twins as individuals. Denise recalls, "My mother never dressed us alike. She was always making distinctions between us. We were disciplined and praised separately. We were not compared as twins."

Because of their curly red hair, Denise and Dorothy were known as the Frizzalight twins. As young children they shared friends, toys, and activities, as well as a secret language. They were separated into different classrooms when they started kindergarten, which was not hard for them because they had been treated as individuals. As school-age children, they had their own individual friends and some cross-over friends. Except for ballet classes, they participated in separate activities outside of school.

Denise, who was the more serious twin, started college earlier than Dorothy. They did not attend the same college because each young woman wanted to develop her own identity and get away from people treating them as a twin pair. Being separated from each other and being away from home was hard. These twins dealt with separation by speaking with each other on the phone every night, discussing their different interests in school and in men.

The girls married within 10 months of each other. Denise was divorced after two years and did not share the pain of her divorce with Dorothy. Denise is now remarried and like Dorothy has three children. Dorothy and Denise are critical of each other's husbands, yet they are able to tolerate each other's choices. They do not believe that they need to see the world in the same way.

Eileen and Jean—Longtime Friends

Eileen and Jean, fraternal twins, were born in a British colony to an educated and business-oriented couple. These girls were welcomed into their family as a very special addition. In turn, Eileen and Jean thought their bond with each other was special. As children they were very close companions and best friends. In spite of the attention they received for being close twins, their parents treated them as individuals. They were encouraged to have their own interests and their own friends and never dressed alike. As children they remember that they were treated differently because of their different personalities. Eileen was more serious and intense, whereas Jean was more relaxed and social.

These girls were separated in kindergarten. By sixth grade they attended different schools. Jean and Eileen recall missing each other and being happy to be together after school. Because they were so close, Eileen and Jean valued each other's interests, even as young children. They went to different colleges but were always in contact. They eventually consulted with each other on their academic, career, and marriage choices. Both women became helping professionals: Eileen is a social worker and Jean is a teacher. Each has a large family and a reserved relationship with her sister's husband.

Unfortunately, Eileen and Jean were geographically separated from each other in their mid-20s. They bridged the 10,000 miles between them by talking to each other on the phone almost every day for 15 years. In their early 40s each had to separately confront the reality that their relationship had been altered by time and distance. They realized that they had grown apart in spite of their longing to hold on to their twinship.

When I spoke with Eileen, she was 50. She shared with me the pain of taking off her rose-colored glasses and seeing her sister Jean with her faults and a different approach to life. In spite of the rough times being a twin—being overidentified and all-consumed by her fantasy of being a twin—Eileen was still content with her sister and her life experiences. Jean was less affected by the psychological problems she went through as an adult separating from her sister.

Alan and Ron—Caring Individuals

Ron and Alan, identical twins, were born into a family that was "delighted" to have twin children. They agree it was fortunate their parents had a lot of help from their extended family because they required a lot of work. Their parents wanted to raise them as individuals and decided never to call them "the twins." The family worked hard to treat them like regular brothers. As children Ron was quiet and used his left hand, whereas Alan was more outgoing and was right-handed. In other ways they were very similar and enjoyed each other's company.

Ron and Alan were separated in first grade, and each boy was encouraged to have his own interests in and outside of school. They shared friends and each had individual friends. They lived a stereotypical suburban childhood: their mother was a homemaker who took care of her four children, and their father was a hardworking businessman who was home for dinner every night. Holidays were always family celebrations.

Perhaps the calm and structure of their childhood and adolescence allowed Ron and Alan to easily separate from each other when they attended different colleges. Both of these men had always been sensitive to, and annoyed by, the attention they received as young twins by onlookers. As adults Alan and Ron were happy to be separated because they hated people staring at them and asking questions of comparison. Alan said, "I just wanted to be me when I went away to college."

Ron and Alan pursued different careers in business. They gradually dealt with their adult feelings of humiliation when others asked if they were twins. Most interestingly, they believe that a competitive and caring relationship has been crucial to success in their separate lives. They are strong critics of each other when it comes to women. Neither Alan nor Ron has ever married because they have never gotten into the "right" relationship with a woman. As they have grown older, they spend less time together but still remain each other's trusted friend.

Veronica and Natalie—Soul Mates

Natalie and Veronica, identical twins, were treated as individuals by their parents and nannies. Because they were Jews they had to be hidden from the Germans during World War II. After the war their family lived in four different countries. During their traumatic but protected childhood, they insisted on being close to each other and dressing alike, and found comfort in being together because they were very shy.

As teenagers they began to separate from each other when their father reestablished his business in the United States. To overcome their shyness these twins studied acting, performing together and alone. They met their husbands in late adolescence while attending business school and performing. Natalie was, and continues to be, the more outgoing and sociable twin, and Veronica is more thoughtful and shy. Both of these women are highly successful in the entertainment business.

Natalie married 10 months before Veronica and has three children, and Veronica has two children. As with many of the twins I interviewed, each woman was critical of her sister's husband and was very close to her sister's children. Veronica and Natalie have lived separate and distinctive personal lives. At the time of the interview they shared an entertainment business and enjoyed working together. Perhaps their interest in performance as a career has made it easier for them to deal with the attention they receive for being twins in a world of singles. In addition, the traumatic nature of their childhoods can never be erased from their memories. Being together reminds them of what they have lived through.

Robert and Gary—An Accepting Alliance

Robert and Gary were the first-born children of young parents who lived in a rural community. Their mother did not want her sons to be stereotypical look-alike twins. She made every effort to treat them as individuals. Robert and Gary had one sister and two brothers who were also close in age. Because the family was poor, all of the children shared their clothes, toys, and other possessions. Robert and Gary were dressed alike only for some childhood pictures.

In kindergarten they were not separated from each other because they attended a small four-room schoolhouse. Until they were in sixth grade, they were in the same classroom with their sister and other brothers. Robert and Gary remember being treated as individuals in spite of all the family closeness. Robert was closer to his mother and more interested in artistic activities, whereas Gary spent a lot of time with his youngest brother playing sports. Robert was more sensitive and communicative, and Gary was prone to outbursts of temper and had a harder time explaining himself. Both of these youngsters had very different styles of dressing; they never dressed alike as school-age children.

After elementary school the family moved to a larger community and all of the children were separated. Robert and Gary were happy to be separated from each other in school because they had such diverse interests. Gary enjoyed literature, and Robert preferred math and science. These twins shared friends and had individual friends also. Gary was a fine athlete and competed in many out-of-town sports events in high school. Gary left his family to go away to college and study art and dance. Robert stayed near home and attended a community college to study engineering.

Financial constraints limited the visits these twins made to each other during college. Separation came naturally for these twins, although Robert did attend one of Gary's dance performances at college. This visit made Robert uncomfortable because he enjoyed forgetting about being a twin. Both of these siblings preferred giving up their twin identities as young men. Gradually they grew further apart, Gary becoming involved with a male lover, and Robert moved in with his girlfriend.

When their father died of lung cancer, these men became closer again. Robert is very accepting of his brother's homosexuality. Gary knows that Robert understands his sexual identity, and he has never felt that his brother is critical of him. Their mother believes that Gary chose to be gay as a way to be different from Robert. Robert and Gary agree that they always had very different inclinations even as young children.

Liz and Lonnie—Double Action

Lonnie and Liz were born to proud parents who established a strong and close family. These twins were never dressed alike because their mother, who was advised by a psychologically minded pediatrician, wanted them to be individuals.

Liz recalls that she was one size bigger than Lonnie and right-handed. Lonnie recalls that they had very different personalities as young children. Both agree that as early as they can remember they coached each other to succeed at a task.

Liz and Lonnie were separated in kindergarten and throughout their schooling. Liz was a better student and Lonnie had learning problems and became the class clown. After school was over, these twins were back together at their house, sharing friends. Liz and Lonnie remember how much fun they had hanging out with the kids at school and in the neighborhood.

Adolescence created further emotional separation for these twins, along with a competition about identity. Lonnie, who always had difficulty succeeding in school, demonstrated her rebelliousness by dyeing her hair different colors and hanging out with a wild crowd, whereas Liz tried out for the drill team and kept up with more middle-of-the-road friends. Liz and Lonnie agree that they were very competitive in high school.

Liz attended college out of town, and Lonnie stayed at home and went to college. Both girls were happy to be apart. They were tired of the "double association" of twinship. They define double association as "There are the twins! Which one are you? Here they come!"

Both girls were glad to be on their own in their early to mid-20s. They lived in separate cities and visited each other whenever possible, keeping in touch by phone. Lonnie dated several men at one time, whereas Liz was a monogamous dater. Neither twin had married when I spoke with them.

In their 30s these twins were living together and sharing clothes and advice. They had gotten over the rough times and appreciated each other. They enjoy traveling together and giving each other advice about the important issues in their lives. Lonnie feels that she can be totally honest and direct with her sister and never have to walk on eggshells. Liz knows that she can't hide from her sister. They consider each other's feelings before they take action.

Arnold and Cynthia—Distant Relatives

Arnold and Cynthia, boy-girl fraternal twins, were born into a poor and chaotic family. Their father was extremely intelligent but very unrealistic. Their mother was kind but ineffective. Because they were boy-girl twins they naturally were treated differently by their parents and relatives. Unfortunately, these twins were neglected. They remember there being very little food in the house when they were young, and they were forced to share whatever clothes and toys they had. Their mother was high-strung and would explode when she became angry. Their father retreated to his books and unsuccessful business interests.

The twins were separated in kindergarten because Cynthia was a better listener than Arnold, who had serious problems sitting still. Cynthia attended Brownies and Girl Scouts, but Arnold did not want to participate in extracurricular activities. Arnold was close to his older brother, and he remembers hanging out with him as a child. Cynthia played with the girls in the neighborhood and stayed away from her family as much as she could. Cynthia remembers trying to help Arnold with his schoolwork with very little success.

Their mother died of cancer when Cynthia and Arnold were teenagers. The children emotionally took care of their father, who managed to support the family by making a few good business deals. Cynthia was sent to college because she was a very good student. Arnold had to get a job and make enough money to support his own college education.

As they grew older, these twins grew further and further apart. At the time of this interview they had been estranged for 15 years. They were not particularly upset about the distance between them, because they didn't remember ever feeling especially close. Perhaps Arnold and Cynthia wanted to get as much distance as possible from each other because being together reminded them of their abusive childhood.

Julie and Greg—A Sibling Bond

Greg and Julie grew up in a middle-class family who were pleased, but financially overwhelmed, by extra children. They were always treated as individuals because they were boy-girl twins. Julie remembers always being with Greg as a child. Greg remembers being punished for Julie's mistakes and getting into trouble for causing problems with Julie.

These children were separated in kindergarten because they had different interests, strengths, and levels of maturity. They eventually began to make separate friends. Julie was close to her mother and sister, and she had many girlfriends. Greg was close to his father and brother and played sports with his teammates. In spite of having separate friends, Julie and Greg stayed close to each other.

When their parents divorced, Julie and Greg were old enough to take sides. Greg was his father's advocate, and Julie was on her mother's side. Gradually different alliances as teenagers created distance between Julie and Greg, who see each other at social events for the family.

Julie is a teacher who has twin children. Greg is in advertising and is unmarried. They describe their relationship as close siblings.

CONCLUSIONS

None of the twins in this study wanted to hold on to their childhood look-alike identity. Each struggled with developing her own identity, as any single person would. The life stories summarized in this chapter display the diversity of adaptions that twins can make. The unique circumstances that each twin pair confronted enhanced, rather than diminished, each person's capacity to become a highly functional individual.

4

Too Close for Comfort?
Issues of Adult Twins

LIVING SEPARATE LIVES

Twins face the triumphs, trials, and lingering after-effects of a childhood shared as each begins a separate life. The cuteness of having an ever-present companion and the attention of curious onlookers wears thin. An adult twin has to learn to live without her sister to function somewhat normally in the world. A twin must give up the companionship of his best friend and counselor if he is to be taken seriously at work and in adult relationships. Although it was acceptable, even entertaining, to have one's twin accompany oneself everywhere as a child or adolescent, this behavior does not seem appropriate in everyday adult life. Of course, some twins don't want to conform to social and psychological standards, so they continue to dress alike and do everything together. These types of twins do not interact much with the non-twin world and the ones I asked chose not to be a part of this study. While conducting this research, I approached three sets of adult twins who lived together. They were interested in knowing about the research I was doing but they all refused to participate in an interview.

Adult twins come to understand that they are different than single children. Twins are born "married" and share so much of their lives that growing apart is difficult and perhaps traumatic. The breakup of a marriage of twins is inevitable, not because the closeness of twinship is abnormal or dysfunctional, but because of its limited value in the realm of adulthood. Part of growing up is learning to find what is meaningful to you alone, separate from your siblings and your friends. Although single children begin to learn this during adolescence because, ideally, it is the focus of the parenting they receive, twins can be delayed in the development of their distinctiveness as individuals.

As twins gradually develop separate lives, they rely on each other less readily. Adulthood is a time when a twin must develop and enhance the identity she has chosen through academic interests, career choice, and marriage or other serious relationships. In her quest to establish a distinctive identity she has many strengths that single children do not have. Twins are naturally attentive and caring, they enjoy the closeness and company of other people, and they generally tend to gravitate toward others because they are not particularly comfortable being alone.

The twins I interviewed were serious, enthusiastic, and competitive in their careers and relationships. Although being energetic and communicative with other people is a highly positive aspect of growing up as a twin, the downside is a vulnerability to exploitation. Because sharing is second nature, adult twins oftentimes do not understand when they are overextending themselves with others. What is appropriate behavior with a twin could be inappropriate with a friend.

As adult twins look back on their childhoods, they perceive on a subconscious and conscious level that their relationship with their twin sibling was too close for comfort. This profound understanding affects their adult life. For example, a twin can be preoccupied with how he is treated by others, or he can take care of another person, say, a lover, as if she were his twin. Because twins become too comfortable with closeness, anger and disappointment with other adults who fail to treat them as carefully and attentively as their twin can be a serious problem.

COMMON PROBLEMS OF ADULT TWINS

Longings for Twinlike Relationships

Adult twins long for the closeness of twinship when they are adults and are separated from their sister or brother. They seek out intense relationships with others, and they may feel misunderstood by the way new people in their lives treat them. When adult twins expect others to be as attentive as their co-twin, they need to learn that others simply do not have the capacity or desire to be close. What can result from this kind of misunderstanding is withdrawal and regression on the twin's part, and feeling ignored or mistreated by other people.

Only after many years of disappointing relationships do twins learn that it is difficult to find someone who is as concerned with intense relationships as they are. As a method of dealing with intense feelings of loneliness, it is quite common for twins to make strong commitments to artistic endeavors, sports, or a business to sublimate the loss of their childhood twinship. Academic pursuits and careers also serve to take the place of the intensity of twinship.

An Inability to Form Reciprocal Relationships with Others in Early Adulthood

Adult twins have serious problems establishing reciprocal relationships with others in their 20s. They struggle with understanding who they are and how much they must give to a new relationship with another. Most interestingly, they turn to their twin to help them sort out what is appropriate with new people and how to form a balance of power with others. Gradually, the problems of give and take with newcomers becomes less intense as twins enter their 30s, but the vulnerability to feeling misunderstood by others remains a lifelong issue.

Many twins agreed with a statement made by a twin who is a psychologist. "I have covert expectations that others will understand me." Her husband's reply, early in their marriage, was "I cannot understand what you are thinking; you have to tell me. I am not your twin."

Being a Twin in a Non-twin World

Adult twins must make up for lost time if they are going to be competitive with colleagues who are not twins. This can be an interesting problem for twins who are used to competing with each other, but the rules are different with non-twins. New non-twin competitors are more cutthroat than their twin sibling, but usually not as skilled in the art of competition. Twins gradually learn how to compete and hold their own in the non-twin world.

Although it is adorable and attention-getting to walk around with one's twin as a child, it is oftentimes annoying and embarrassing to be an adult twin in a non-twin world. Onlookers' questions about who is taller, smarter, friendlier, prettier, richer, more popular, or better-traveled seem pointless. Adult twins know that these questions are superficial and disingenuous and more often than not just a reaction to seeing two people who look alike. If an onlooker is genuinely concerned with, say, the way competition has been handled between twins, it is still inappropriate to ask these questions in public of someone you don't know.

Most twins try to avoid public situations together as adults. They don't enjoy being the evening's entertainment, a spontaneous horse and pony show, or show-and-tell. Onlookers create problems for twins that their parents could never imagine. Family members, including parents, aunts, uncles, grandparents, cousins, and children, are usually sensitive to problems created by comparisons. They are less concerned with the similarities and differences between their twin relatives, which makes public appearances with family members less troublesome.

My own children are very tuned in to the interaction I have with my twin sister. It is as if they have entered my twin world. They know the power of her anger and the contentment we share when we are in agreement, as well as the acute anxiety when we are both upset. I think all twins can identify with these statements.

The power of two in a non-twin world is substantial, even amazing. After twins separate, they can reconnect with an astonishing sense of togetherness that non-twins cannot understand. Their own history together gives them confidence and empathy for each other that is hard to put into words.

Twins Want to Re-create Their Twinship with Others

Adult twins often want to form an attachment that replicates or replaces their childhood twin relationship. Whether this longing is conscious or unconscious, adult twins look for and manage to form intense relationships with others. Usually it takes a great deal of energy and a lot of fine-tuning to develop a closeness with another person that is satisfying for a twin. A twin is willing to work hard to find a soul mate because she finds casual relationships boring or difficult to understand.

Marriage, for most of the twins I interviewed, was a way to fill in the gap of loneliness created by being separated from their twin in adulthood. Children of twins served as unconscious twin replacements for many of the adults who participated in this study.

COMMON PATTERNS IN ADULT RELATIONSHIPS

Adult Twins Established Distinctive Relationships

Most adult twins developed separate and distinct relationships with others that did not include or even interest their twin sister or brother. They chose very different husbands or wives. Interestingly, husbands and wives were often critical of their spouse's twin, although they might have a genuine affection for the co-twin as well. Many of the twins I spoke with talked openly about how hard it was for their husband or wife to accept the emotional closeness that they shared with their twin.

None of the twins I spoke with felt that hostility between their spouse and their twin sibling would jeopardize the twin relationship or their marriage. Criticism of one's partner was acceptable, predictable, and understandable, given the intensity of the twin relationship growing up.

Adult Twins Established Distinctive Lifestyles

Although adult twins kept in contact and had some curiosity about each other's lifestyles, they did not show any interest in being a copy of each other or a half of a whole person. Twins who shared similar interests also had many different interests. In fact, having similar lifestyles seemed to be avoided because it drew attention to the twinship and distracted twins from having an individual identity.

Adult Twins Developed Distinctive Family Relationships

Relationships with parents, sisters, and brothers changed as twins grew up. The closeness that a twin shared with their mother, father, sister, or brother was different from the closeness with their twin sibling. Adult twins did not feel jealous of the different family relationships that were established after childhood. They were open, as well as curious, about how different family members had formed different alliances. For example, one twin of the pair would identify more closely with his mother. This identification with the mother could be seen clearly in life choices such as marriage and careers, or in some cases, in sexuality.

Adult Twins Found Parenting to Be Meaningful

Seventy percent of the twins I spoke with were parents. They had strong connections to their children, who seemed on some conscious and unconscious level to be re-creations of their twin relationship. If they had twins, they raised them to be individuals even if they had not had this experience growing up. In general, twins' attitudes toward parenting seemed to be similar and intense.

Adult Twins Come to Terms with Developmental Distinctiveness

Although during their 20s and 30s twins may have resented the fact that they had a co-twin, by middle age they came to accept the good aspects, bad qualities, and weirdness related to twinship. Even twins with a split identity were able to get some perspective on how twinship had affected them, and they were able to move on to new relationships and a new sense of themselves.

Adult Twins Are Highly Empathetic Individuals

Twins are effective in relationships with other people because they learned the value of attentiveness and caring from their twin sibling. They are loyal to their friends and like to share intimate aspects of themselves, rather than presenting themselves in a superficial manner. This capacity for empathy led many in this study to seek out careers as mental health professionals, doctors, or teachers. Creativity, a combination of empathy with cognitive flexibility, led many of them to become actors, dancers, designers, writers, and painters.

COMPOSITE OF YOUNG ADULT TWINSHIP

Imagine the following scenario of Beatrice and Maggie as adults. After graduating from college, Beatrice has a small informal wedding with 50 close friends. Six months later Maggie has a large formal wedding for 200 guests. Their weddings highlight their distinctiveness. Beatrice marries a professor and has a literary, old-fashioned ceremony followed by a party at her mother's house. Maggie marries a businessman in a religious contemporary ceremony followed by a fancy reception at a hotel. Even though they have different ideas and tastes, they enjoy being at each other's weddings because they still share and cherish each other's feelings.

Beatrice and Maggie move to different cities hundreds of miles apart. They are now used to being separated and enjoy swapping stories about their different experiences. Beatrice is a teacher and loves to cook. Maggie is working for an art dealer and loves to travel. Both still like to talk about clothes, and they look forward to getting together so they can swap possessions. They are both planning to have families as soon as possible, and they want to have their own homes to decorate and care for.

Beatrice doesn't like Maggie's husband because she thinks he is too interested in money and getting ahead. He expects Maggie to go to many parties with him. Maggie doesn't respect Beatrice's husband, whom she describes as an intellectual phony. Maggie thinks he is not practical enough to create a stable home for her sister. The girls fight and then talk, talk and then fight about the best way for each of them to have the best life possible. Their parents and husbands are amused by the intensity of their arguments about how to live life.

Another aspect of their relationship consists of telephone conversations. Maggie and Beatrice talk to each other two or three times a week. They just seem to like talking about everything from politics to friends, clothes, cars, and summer vacations. Phone calls seem to make their separation more tolerable. Their phone calls also help them understand their strengths when meeting new people, as well as what is difficult about it. Maggie gives advice and insight to Beatrice about the parents of kids in her class, new friends she shares with her husband, and an old high school buddy who is depressed. In turn Beatrice advises Maggie on how to develop the collection at the gallery and how to get along with her pushy boss. She has insights about why it is hard for Maggie to get along with her husband's wealthy friends. Occasionally they have arguments that last for days or weeks. They usually make up after an important problem arises that one of them needs advice about.

As the years go by, they occasionally—at least twice a year—visit each other's homes and meet each other's friends. They hate shopping alone, but they also hate shopping together, because everyone stares at them and asks foolish questions. They agree to stop shopping together when they visit. Beatrice and Maggie have made the transition to adulthood and no longer feel special for being twin sisters. Their relationship is focused on trust and sharing. They try to be soul mates who help each other through the good times and bad times.

UNIQUE EXPERIENCES OF ADULT TWINS

Most of the adult twins who participated in this study went through the common experiences described above. The pattern of twinship, be it unit identity, interdependent identity, split identity, or individual identity, did not affect how motivated twins were about establishing separate and distinct lives. There were differences between the patterns of twinship in terms of the capacity to form new relationships outside the twinship. Unit identity and interdependent identity twins were very dependent on each other and remained best friends. Split identity twins gradually learned to deal with their conflicts. They grew further and further apart as the decades of their lives passed by. They never resolved their conflicts, and were likely to suffer from loneliness. Individual identity twins dealt more matter-of-factly with each other. They remained close and trusted friends but were able to expand their social network to other people.

Unique struggles or traumatic life experiences faced all twins. The following sections include their reactions to inordinate or unusual stress.

Divorce

Approximately 50% of the sample survived divorce. This statistic mirrors the divorce rate for the general population, as reported by the U.S. Census Bureau in 2002. Twins from all the patterns of twinship experienced this emotional disaster as young adults or in their midlives. Divorce was discussed and accepted by both members of the twin pair. It was not a source of contention or undue criticism; in most cases twins reached out to their sibling to support them emotionally and financially, if necessary. When one twin became single, it was common for both to rekindle their togetherness. For example, twins felt it was normal to invite their single twin to have dinner every night or to travel together for a vacation. This rekindling of closeness was done whether or not their spouse was supportive of this behavior.

Cancer

Four sets of twins were faced with one member having a potentially life-threatening cancer. Their stories are summarized below.

Cathy and Carol, identical interdependent identity twins, faced the horror of cancer when Carol was 34. Carol, the strong or dominant twin, received a diagnosis of breast cancer and had a mastectomy followed by one year of chemotherapy. This was a terrifying experience for her. Her sister Cathy recalls what a difficult time it was for both of them. Cathy worried that because she was an identical twin, she was more likely to contract cancer also. In addition, these twins reported that when one of them suffers, they both suffer. Fortunately, Cathy never got a cancer diagnosis and Carol has been in remission for 30 years.

These twins confronted cancer together. Cathy helped Carol begin the rehabilitation process. Carol took her rehabilitation so seriously that she was asked to help other cancer survivors deal with their recovery, developing new programs on coping strategies.

Candy and Serena, fraternal twins with an interdependent identity, each faced cancer at different times in their lives. Serena received a thyroid cancer diagnosis at 35. Her sister was instrumental in her recovery process, providing emotional and hands-on help.

In her early 50s, Cathy got a diagnosis of a more serious form of lung cancer that had spread. At the time of writing this book, Candy's cancer was in remission, but the prognosis for her survival was not hopeful. Serena made 10 cross-country trips to be with Candy through surgeries and chemotherapy. Serena said, "It felt like I was going crazy. I felt like I was going to lose my mind. I was crying all the time." Serena entered psychotherapy for the first time in her life to understand her reaction to the looming death of her twin sister.

Candy spoke with me about her sadness and deep concern for her sister. I believe she feared that Serena's identity was so intertwined with her own that her death would create a serious loss to Serena's sense of herself. Joan Woodward in *The Lone Twin* (1998) describes this type of loss of self as part of the bereavement experience of twins.

One set of identical twins both survived cancer. Emily and Deena, identical split identity twins, were well into midlife when both got a breast cancer diagnosis within a three-year period. Although these twins had a distant and turbulent relationship, they showed concern for each other's well-being. They were the most supportive of each other during this time when their lives were in jeopardy, exchanging pertinent information about the nature and progress of their illnesses and discussing treatment options extensively.

Bob and Al, identical twin brothers, faced the threat of cancer in midlife when Bob got kidney cancer. His only hope for survival was a transplant from a donor whose tissues matched his. Although these twins lived separate lives and seemed to have a distant relationship with each other, Al flew across the country and gave his brother one of his kidneys. Bob survived the transplant surgery and returned to work, and the prognosis is excellent for total remission of his cancer.

All four sets of twins provided emotional support and attention to each other throughout their battles with cancer. Their interactions reflect deep concern for each other's well-being.

Bulimia and Anorexia

Twins with interdependent and split identities reported having eating disorders because of a desire to be thin and as a means of establishing an identity separate from their twin. The influence or support of the twin sibling when one of the pair was troubled by this mental disorder was not important to eventual resolution of the problem. A twin's obsession with weight as a way of establishing separateness was dangerous and destructive to the twin herself as well as harmful to the bond with her twin.

Cindy and Debbie, split identity twins, were born and raised in a beach community. Debbie was the favored twin and Cindy was considered the bad one. They both developed a serious eating disorder, anorexia, in adolescence. They have both remained extremely thin their entire lives and are unable to overcome their obsession with food. Psychotherapy to deal with their eating disorders has not been successful.

Mary developed anorexia as a teenager. Melinda spent years trying to get her sister to realize she had an eating disorder, without any success. Mary was highly resistant to giving up her strange and damaging eating patterns. Eventually Melinda gave up hope of helping her sister, who continued her self-destructive behavior into her adulthood. Mary has entered psychotherapy in her late 40s to get over her eating problems, but Melinda thinks she has waited too long and that her overall health and longevity have been compromised.

Loss of a Twin

Two sets of fraternal twins were faced with the death of their twin sibling. Both of these women were emotionally devastated by this experience and shared their stories of loss with me.

Ann and Arlene have been discussed in earlier chapters. They shared an interdependent identity bond because of child abuse and neglect. Ann, the stronger twin, survived to tell her story of life after her sister's suicide at age 25. Ann still believes her sister did not mean to kill herself, and she gets comfort from her belief.

Holding on to the memory of her twinship, Ann lived for 10 years with a "hole in her chest." She raised four children and worked to develop her own career. At the age of 35, she began intensive psychotherapy, which lasted five years and helped her understand and work through her grief. At the time of writing this book, Ann had never again attempted to be close to another adult. Her story reflects Woodward's (1998) hypothesis on the loss of a twin: "If the loss of the twin has been in early adulthood they may have difficulties forming a very close relationship again as it can feel like a betrayal of a twin who died, or that no one can match the relationship that they had with their twin" (p. 73).

When I spoke with Ann before the publication of this book, she was very involved with her teenage children and was a successful businesswoman. She suffered from social anxiety and was still reluctant to form an intimate relationship with someone besides her children, although she hoped one day to open her heart to someone else.

Nancy and Terry, fraternal twins with an individual identity bond, were faced with the imminent death of one of the twin pair. Terry was born with a congenital heart problem, and her life expectancy was very short. Nancy was aware of her sister's heart condition from the time she was eight years old. Both twins were prepared for separation from each other because of death.

Nancy adapted to the loss of her sister at age 10 and managed to move on with her life. She has worked for many years with twins who have lost their twin sibling. In this way she stays connected emotionally to her lost sister. Woodward writes about the need for twins to hold on to the spirit of their twin as a way to ward off loneliness (1998).

Loss of a Child

One twin I interviewed lost her son to suicide. Her twin sister was supportive during the long years of his mental illness as a youth. All of the extended family provided financial help and emotional support. As an adult this individual decided to take his own life. His mother and her twin sister dealt with this tragic loss together and became even closer.

Loss of a Parent

All the twins with whom I spoke spent time together when one of their parents passed away. During times like these twins rekindled the closeness they shared, as they found strength and comfort in being together. This reaction is similar to sisters and brothers who are not twins.

Serious Family Illness

Many of the twins I interviewed worked together with their twin when there was a serious illness in the family, whether or not they shared a close relationship in their daily lives. This reaction, too, is similar to sisters and brothers who are not twins.

Mental Illness

One set of identical twins suffered from a serious mood disorder that was manifested in early adulthood. The precursors to this mental illness were apparent when Carrie and Charlene were children. Primarily outgoing and expressive, they would at times become withdrawn and fearful. Their parents tried to make distinctions between the girls and wanted to respect their individuality. In addition, Charlene and Carrie wanted to be their own people. These twins fall into the category of sharing an individual identity.

Charlene developed as the leader or more dominant twin. She was impulsive, defiant, and high-strung, whereas Carrie was friendly and less out of control than Charlene. Both girls found themselves getting into trouble with drugs and law enforcement because they were unable to internalize or contain their anger. As teenagers they formed a gang and threatened other girls, using the power of their twinship for intimidation. They valued being tough and aggressive in their adolescence.

These girls developed three distinct ways of dealing with each other that reflected serious emotional issues related to a major mood disorder. First, Charlene and Carrie were competitive with each other in many areas, including friends, sports, and grades. Second, they were too compassionate and over-identified with each other's mood swings, which caused serious disruptions in both women's capacity to function. Finally, Carrie and Charlene could be antagonistic and mean to each other, preying on the other's weakness. For example, Charlene would call Carrie "the evil twin" and Carrie would call Charlene "the bitch" when they were angry with each other.

By the age of 20, both girls had suffered from a major depression after living through the breakup of a relationship with a boyfriend. Charlene said, "The depression brought us closer together. I could express what was bothering my twin sister when she was unable to explain it for herself. When we are both depressed at the same time, it is horrible. When we both feel weak, it is very hard for us to function."

Carrie spoke with me at length about her problems with depression and hypomania. "I've gone through some hard times. I've been bipolar. I've been high and down. It took a long time to piece it together. My sister and I have gone through intense times because we share the same genetics and family history. But we are still individuals with different souls."

Carrie and Charlene agree that they have problems with moodiness. Continues Charlene, "My problems are different because my self-esteem is higher. Carrie lets herself get overwhelmed and is not as aware of the dangers of depression as I am." Charlene and Carrie have been in psychotherapy since they were adolescents to deal with emotional issues related to their mood disorder as well as their twinship. Mental illness has brought these twins closer to each other, but it has also contributed to the confusion of their identities and to the way they share each other's pain.

Divergent Sexual Orientation

Three sets of male twins discovered different sexual orientations in adolescence. Following is a brief synopsis of their experiences with the coming-out process and how their twin reacted to this information.

Kevin and Kyle, identical twins, were the youngest children in a large wealthy family. They remember that they were treated as individuals by their parents, who welcomed the boys into the world. Kevin remembers as a very young child that his father teased him more than Kyle. Kyle was the more athletic twin, who was closer to his father. Kevin was the more artistic and sensitive twin, who was closer to his mother.

Kyle and Kevin were separated in kindergarten. They dressed differently and had different friends and interests. They remember being very good friends as children and as adolescents. Both boys left home at age 16 to go their separate ways. When Kevin shared with Kyle that he was homosexual, Kyle was very accepting of his brother's sexual orientation. Kyle told me in a very affectionate way that his brother could be weird but not because he was gay. Kevin finds his brother's "butch" lifestyle "interesting, but not for me." Kevin accepts Kyle's lifestyle, which includes supporting his family as a contractor.

When their parents passed away within three years of each other, Kyle and Kevin spent extended time together. Kyle named one of his three children after his brother. Kevin told me that his brother and his family are always welcome in his home. These men do not seem to have any reservations about each other. Both believe that Kevin's homosexuality could be related to his close alliance with his mother.

Robert and Gary, identical twins, were the firstborn children of raspberry farmers in the Northwest. They are identical twins who share an individual identity bond. They have three younger siblings who are all very close in age. Their childhood and adolescence was spent in a rural community.

Both twins remember that their mother did not want them to be stereotyped as twins. Each child was treated as an individual and encouraged to establish his own interests. Gary was more athletic than Robert, who was more sensitive and more like his mother.

These boys are dressed alike as young children in photographs but established their own personal styles early in life. They attended a four-room schoolhouse and were often in the same classroom until they were in sixth grade. In middle school and high school Gary became competitive in sports while Robert developed interest in art and dance.

Gary and Robert were separated when they attended college. Robert studied dance and Gary studied engineering. Gary was surprised when his brother told him that he was gay because Robert had dated women in high school. There was no criticism or conflict over Robert's sexual orientation. His family discussed his coming-out with him. Gary was the most supportive member of the family in regard to Robert's homosexuality. Gary wondered if he might have homosexual tendencies himself, although he had never been attracted to a man.

Colin and Craig, fraternal twins, were the oldest sons in a religious family. Their mother and father were in their early 30s when their twins were born. Both parents "loved" having twins, wanted their children to be treated as individuals, and were careful to treat them equally. Their mother never wanted them to be treated as a pair, and the children were dressed in the same outfits only for family pictures. Differences were apparent at birth. Colin was more sensitive and quiet, and Craig was more outgoing, negative, and outspoken. In spite of their differences, these boys were always very close.

The family was not doing well financially when the twins were young, and they moved throughout three states in the Midwest so that their father could find work. Colin and Craig had two younger sisters before the family settled in Seattle, where the boys attended a private Christian school for grades K–12. Their differences were apparent to others who were close to them. They never dressed alike and were always separated in school. Colin remembers that he always felt like an outsider at school, whereas Craig seemed to fit in better. Craig was interested in sports and Colin was more artistically inclined. These twins relied on each other throughout their childhood and adolescence. They moved away from home at the same time and shared a car to attend different colleges. Colin studied fashion design and Craig studied business.

Colin, the insecure twin, had more difficulty being separated from his brother when they attended college. At 20 he entered therapy to deal with feeling overwhelmed and insecure without his brother. Soon thereafter Colin realized that he felt like he didn't fit in because he was gay. Psychotherapy helped Colin work on his poor self-esteem. Gradually he shared with his brother that he was gay. Craig had serious problems accepting his brother's discovery.

These twins have had a great deal of difficulty talking openly about sexuality. Colin believes that Craig is not critical of his orientation and that he is sensitive to his feelings. Craig would not comment on his brother's homosexuality.

Repressed Memories

Mary and Melinda shared a split identity bond, so they were eager to go their separate ways when the opportunity was presented to them in college. Marriage and the demands of young adulthood created more distance between these twins, who lived in different cities and pursued different careers and lifestyles. Mary was more free-spirited and adventurous, whereas Melinda was more serious and concerned about financial security. As the years passed, these women became extremely alienated from each other. Melinda was afraid of Mary's criticism of her lifestyle, thinking Mary did not accept her choices. Mary was annoyed by Melinda's worrisome nature, her inability to just have fun.

Although they never discussed why they couldn't get along, they both knew that keeping a distance both physically and emotionally was the best way to cope with their disagreements. From their mid-20s to 40s they hardly spoke to each other, which was a relief for both of them. Their children did not see each other or attend family parties together. Their parents, husbands, and children accepted their alienation from each because they witnessed their pain when they did spend time together.

In midlife Melinda began psychoanalysis to deal with her strong feelings of loneliness and depression. Being in psychoanalysis stirred up many repressed memories, and she began to have flashbacks of early sexual abuse. She felt tortured by these memories and reached out to Mary for help in recalling the details of what had happened. Mary agreed to be Melinda's memory bank. These women rekindled their relationship in the hope of putting together a coherent picture of their childhood and resolving their anger, frustration, and disappointments with each other.

Mary was able to share details of her childhood memories that Melinda had repressed, forgotten, or had never remembered experiencing. Mary's recollections helped Melinda remember in greater detail aspects of the sexual abuse that she had forgotten, in locations such as the family business. While Melinda was getting in touch with her incestuous experiences, Mary remained certain that she herself had not been sexually abused.

As painful as this was for both women, Melinda's forgotten memories brought them together for almost five years. The intensity of discomfort related to these incestuous memories was so difficult to bear that Mary and Melinda needed each other to digest and process what had happened to them in early childhood. Although Mary still firmly believes that she was not a part of the sexual perversions that occurred, Melinda silently thinks that Mary is also a victim of incest.

Unfortunately, misunderstandings and personality differences have once again created a wedge between Mary and Melinda. They are now, again, estranged. At best, their attempt to piece together their past brought more equality to their relationship. Mary has come to realize that she is not all good and that she has made her own mistakes and that she has regrets. Melinda sees herself in a more positive light.

CONCLUSION

Countless shared experiences in childhood can lead to unique adult problems for twins. Although a sense of security can result, the intense closeness is difficult to replicate in the adult world. A twin commonly longs for someone to share her emotional life because this process reaffirms her sense of self as being worthy and understandable. The need to be affirmed and understood is as compelling as the need to be close to one's twin.

In spite of the difficulties in relinquishing twinship, adult twins separate and form very distinctive lives. They marry and have children and careers. Some twins remain best friends, some twins argue endlessly, and other twins manage to work out their issues with each other. The problem of being overly close is gradually resolved with time and expansive life experiences. By the time twins reach middle age, their bond is more similar to that of brothers and sisters than it was in their infancy, childhood, adolescence, and young adulthood.

5

The Twinning Bond

IS THERE A DEFINITION OF THE TWIN BOND?

Obviously there is no precise way to define the bond twins share. When I ask twins themselves, they answer with statements such as, "I've always been a twin, so how can I understand how my relationship with my twin is different from that of a single child?" "The experience of growing up as a twin and the bond we share wouldn't be so hard to understand if everyone were born a twin." "Everyone agrees the twin bond is different from a sibling bond."

Nevertheless, there is a variety of theoretical descriptions of what constitutes the twinning bond. Psychologists believe the bond between twins begins in utero and develops, consciously and unconsciously, throughout the twins' lives, so that there is a thread connecting them emotionally. This deep connection in young children includes a need for their twin sibling in times of stress, the exquisite comfort of being together, and patterns or ways of communicating with each other that are spoken and unspoken and difficult for others to understand. The twin bond often includes a heightened sense of telepathy or extrasensory perception (Malmstrom & Poland, 1999; Perlman & Gannon, 2000; Schave & Ciriello, 1983).

The most obvious basis for the existence of a bond between identical twins is their similar genetic, environmental, and parental input. Fraternal twins share this lifelong bond as well, which suggests that environment and parenting style are very strong determinants. The twin bond resembles the sibling bond, but is much more intense. Whether or not this bond can be measured, it clearly exists because of the circumstances of close birth and growing up together (Zazzo, 1960).

A different way of perceiving the bond between twins is to describe it as a mutual dependency: "The twinning reaction consists of mutual interidentification and part fusion of the self representation and the object's representation of the other member of the pair. This leads to a difference of ego boundaries between two people. This reaction may occur in siblings who are relatively close together in age, or it may occur between a couple married for a period of time" (Tabor & Joseph, 1961, p. 277).

Tabor, as well as other psychoanalysts, thinks the twinning process involves a psychological belief that you are a part of the other person, that there is a distribution or a shared sense of self between a pair of twins or close individuals. This unconscious, partial merging of identities is not considered disruptive or unusual to a young pair of twins. In fact, researchers have described twin language, such as the use of "we" for "me," as an example of partially merged identities (Koch, 1966). The effects of shared identity lead to a special closeness, a sense of belonging.

An exaggerated sense of belonging to each other is a simple but accurate way to describe the twinning bond. Psychoanalysts go on in more detail about the twin bond and speculate that it is based on early identification with each other (Burlingham, 1952; Leonard, 1961; Tabor & Joseph, 1961). Identification is defined as

the most primitive method of recognizing external reality; it is, in fact, nothing less than mental mimicry. Its necessary preconditions are unbroken narcissism, which cannot bear that anything should exist outside itself, and the weakness of the individual, which makes him unable to annihilate his environment or take flight from it. The child then uses identification to transform what is strange and frightening in the external world into what is familiar and enjoyable. (Hinsie & Campbell, 1970, p. 373)

According to psychoanalysts, identification between twins—the twin bond—often slows down the motivation of both individuals in the pair to separate, and confusion with self-image and identity are inevitable. This primary inter-twin identification may complicate the development of a healthy and separate self (Scheinfeld, 1967). Leonard (1961) suggests that the dependency of one twin on the other often causes self-images to remain blurred. It is the blurring of self-images that leads to identity confusion.

Burlingham (1952) observed that twins who came from low socioeconomic backgrounds with a very similar physical appearance and parental or cultural attitudes that did not stress individuality often experience severe problems in language development and ego development. Burlingham's observations seem to be reflective of what I have labeled as the unit identity twin bond and the interdependent identity twin bond.

Farber (1981) retrospectively analyzed 100 sets of twins separated at birth and reared apart. Farber believed that the twin bond was a manifestation of intra-psychic conflict between twins over individuality. Farber saw striving for individuality in twins as more crucial than genetics or environment. She writes,

Overall, the findings underscore the significance of individuality. If twins reared in even moderately different homes remain markedly alike, what more do we need in order to acknowledge the genetic uniqueness of each individual? Similarly, if twins make themselves "artificially" different as a result of contact with each other, what more do we need to indicate the need of each individual to be an individual, separate unto himself and clearly bounded! (p. 53)

Other researchers who have measured dependency between twins suggested that the twin bond—the psychological thread between twins—affects personality development (Paluszny & Gibson, 1974; Paluszny & Beht-Hallahni, 1974; Vandenberg & Wilson, 1979; Schave, 1982; Schave & Ciriello, 1983). These researchers suggest that the twin bond is not a transient psychological phenomenon. Rather, the twin bond affects adult development.

The resolution or disappearance of this psychological thread between twins is impossible. Once a twin, always a twin. Even though it is elusive and perhaps immeasurable by conventional means, the twin bond is a crucial part of development throughout the lives of twins.

PATTERNS OF TWINSHIP

The pattern of twinship or the type of twinning bond that twins share is determined by the quality of parenting that twins receive in their infancy and early childhood (Schave & Ciriello, 1983). The twinning bond is a primary relationship originating at the conception of the individual and evolving as a compensatory and complementary relationship alongside the development of the mother-child bond. All the participants in my original study of 40 sets of identical and fraternal twins were able to describe a primary bond between themselves and their twin (Schave & Ciriello, 1983). All 30 sets of identical and fraternal twins who participated in my current study were able to describe a primary bond that was at least as significant or more significant than the mother-child bond.

See Table 5.1 for a summary of the relationship between patterns of twinship and the twin bond.

Intertwined Lives: Unit Identity

Identical twins who shared a unit identity twin bond were very closely connected to each other because of parental neglect and extremely stressful events, such as being incarcerated in a concentration camp. There was a common theme of seeking attention in the earliest memories of these twins. They remember "being dressed up and put on stage to perform" or "attracting attention because there were two of us." Or a sense of close connection: "She was always there, like another leg in my crib."

When reflecting upon the meaning of the bond with his brother, Henry said, "The bond is a very powerful force in my life. It has influenced us in ways we don't understand but serves to make us feel never totally alone in the world." His twin, Harry, added, "The bond between us is inevitable, making our lives interrelated. It is larger than the two of us and cannot be overcome."

Table 5.1
TheTwin Bond

Pattern of Twinship	Early Relationship	Adult Relationship
Unit Identity	Indistinguishable from each other Symbiotic tie	Powerful Inevitable closeness Enmeshment
Interdependent Identity	Joined at the hip Overly concerned about each other	Accept each other with a blind faith Need to share thoughts, feelings and relationships
Split Identity	Ambivalent relationship Feel like freaks Burdened by twin Look forward to separation	Dramatic intense conflicts Relieved to be apart Distant estranged relationship
Individual Identity	Individuality attended to by parents Encouraged to separate	Realistic trust for each other Deep concern for each other's well-being

Ida and Eleanor described their bond to each other as a crucial life force. Ida said, "We started together and we stayed together. Now we have our independence with our husbands and families. Later on we will be back together." Eleanor added, "There isn't anything we can't share."

The bond between these two sets of unit identity twins demonstrates what a powerful and all-pervasive type of relationship they share. Unit identity twins' lives are so intertwined that most likely they do not develop an autonomous sense of self.

Blind Faith: Interdependent Identity

Identical and fraternal twins who share an interdependent bond are totally accepting of each other. These twins understand each other's limitations or differences from each other without criticism. Interdependent identity twins tolerate each other's idiosyncrasies. This remarkable acceptance of a twin is not present in the other, more-evolved twin bond patterns. The interdependent bond is all-encompassing psychologically. These twins are highly dependent on each other for emotional support because they have never developed a deep attachment to their mother or father. Their twin is the most trusted person in their life; their bond excludes others from being as important to them as their twin sibling is. Spouses and children are second best to their twin and are on some unconscious level shared by the pair.

The earliest memories of these twins includes the close presence of the twin: "I remember always being a twin and always being together." "I remember people stopping my mother and asking her if we were twins." "I remember lying close to each other in our cribs."

Carol and Cathy, interdependent identity twins who were 42 years old at the time of the study, have always been available for each other. Carol explained, "My sister is the first person I think of when I have a problem. This closeness can't be taken away. The bond is a closeness between us that can't exist with other people." Cathy elaborated, "Our bond has gone through cycles. We were very close as children. We were treated as if we were one person. We were never treated as individuals. When we went to college, we separated for the first time and established different lives. As we have grown older, we have grown close to each other again, even with our separate interests. It feels like she is a part of me. She is my other half. This closeness comes from years and years of sharing our thoughts and feelings."

Fraternal twins Candy and Serena described their bond as a very strong connection. Candy explained, "Our bond means always having her there to share our thoughts and feelings; we share each other's experiences. Our bond is a closeness between us that can't exist with other people." Serena, who knew she was terminally ill at the time of the interview, was very concerned about how her sister would be able to live on her own after her death. As resigned as she was to her own death, she was equally saddened at leaving her sister behind. Serena realized that Candy would have a gaping and unfillable hole in her life when she passed away.

Ann described her bond with Arlene as "right for her. Twins like to resolve their arguments. With Arlene, I could always tell her how I felt because at the end of the day we always had each other—we were a tight unit. We were mothers to each other because our mother was always drunk. We protected each other from loneliness. She was very socially involved, and I was the independent twin. Arlene got too involved with other people for her self-esteem. They disappointed her and she felt like killing herself. She didn't want to be dead for more than a day, I think."

Interdependent twins hold on to their memories of the close presence of their twin. They cannot imagine not being close to their twin. Their relationship to their spouse is second to their twinship. Blind-faith acceptance of each other is the hallmark of this enmeshed bond. Fighting between these twins is "over in a minute."

THE CURSE OF TWINSHIP: SPLIT IDENTITY

Identical and fraternal twins who share a split identity twin bond are highly ambivalent about each other. They have mixed feelings: they sometimes like each other and enjoy being twins, but at other moments they dislike each other intensely and feel disappointed and burdened by each other. They often feel that it is freaky to be a twin. As adults these twins feel that twinship is a curse.

Dramatic conflicts between these polar-opposite twins arise out of the most minor disagreements and turn into major battles. Onlookers are often confused when they see twins who can't get along. An examination of their confused relationship makes the intense struggles of these twins understandable. Most interestingly, twins who have been split into good and bad do not see their bond in the same way. The "good" twin who has been idealized is impervious to the pain her twin experiences from being devalued by her entire family. The good twin sees only what she needs from her sister. She is angry and disappointed when she doesn't get what she wants from her twin. The good twin's perception of the twin bond depends on a moment-to-moment evaluation of her needs from twinship. She can easily write off her twin as bad and uncaring and then return to her for advice and counsel when she feels like she needs something from being a twin. The good, idealized twin's bond with her sister is inconsistent and dependent on her state of mind.

The "bad" twin struggles with her negative sense of self. She is easily subjected to humiliation from others as well as from her twin. The devalued twin suffers from depression because of her unrealistic need to please others. The bad twin's need to please others sabotages her self-esteem and self-worth because she is too preoccupied with what others need and what her sister needs. Finding her own voice and feeling worthy is a long-standing problem for the bad twin.

Separation for split identity twins is imperative and inevitable. They usually separate after high school or college. Both twins miss each other because they are used to having each other to measure themselves against. Upon separation the good twin does not know how to evaluate herself because she can't measure herself against her sister, so she looks for new people to devalue. The bad twin finds a new unrealistic standard for herself.

Melinda described her bond with her sister. "Mary likes being a twin when it suits her purpose or goal—if she can gain something from being with me or being a twin. I feel sorry that my sister is so deceptive and can be so malicious— I feel like I don't even know her when she acts like this. Being a twin has been difficult and humiliating."

Mary said, "Our bond has never been resolved. It's not important that we get along. . . . It's hard for us to be together. We have issues with control.

When I was younger, I wanted to keep Melinda from causing problems, but I couldn't. And now the reality of our lives is more important than our arguments. Our bond of childhood made me more vulnerable and able to be close to other people. We are not close now."

Emily and Deena, identical twins, were polarized into good and bad twins. Emily, the bad twin, said "I was devalued in the family, and I have been in psychoanalysis for many years to get over feeling like the victim. I don't need to feel close to my sister. I don't trust my sister. She uses my feelings to take advantage of me. My feelings are important when we have the same perceptions—when we are in agreement." Emily sees Deena only at weddings and funerals.

Deena spent 20 years in psychotherapy trying to find happiness and meaning in her life. She still longs for her sister Emily to be reasonable and supportive and to take her point of view. Deena still strongly desires the early closeness of twinship, which affirmed her sense of importance.

Cindy and Debbie, polarized identical twins, expressed their ambivalence about being twins in a different way. Debbie, the good or idealized twin, said, "We have a strange relationship—a strange bond. I am always angry that Cindy can't be what I want her to be. We can be so close and creative together when we get along."

Cindy, who was devalued in the family, was always afraid of Debbie's criticism and out-of-control behavior. Cindy found that small doses of her sister were more than enough for her. She moved 5,000 miles away from her family and Debbie. Cindy wanted to spend only two or three days a year with her sister. Cindy thought that separating from her sister freed her to pursue her own life and her own success.

Melinda's earliest memory is crying in kindergarten when Mary spilled paint on herself, because she knew she would get in trouble for Mary's clumsiness or bad behavior. Mary remembers that both girls got in trouble in kindergarten because of spilled paint.

The shared distribution of punishment or criticism when only one twin causes the problem is also seen with interdependent and unit identity twins. However, in a polarized identity twinship, when the devalued twin takes the blame for the idealized twin's problems, a serious developmental issue results. The devalued twin's responsibility is to both members of the pair. The idealized twin takes no responsibility, or as little responsibility as possible. This creates character problems for both twins. The idealized twin is self-centered and lawless—he becomes narcissistic. The devalued twin is masochistic and unrealistic about his faults, which leads to depression. These twins often seek out psychotherapy as adults.

TRUSTED FRIENDS: INDIVIDUAL IDENTITY

Identical and fraternal twins, including male-female pairs, who have received "good enough" parenting and who have been cared for and treated well as individuals by their parents, develop a separate, distinctive sense of self. As adults they feel a special bond of trust with their twin sibling based on shared memories and experiences. However, they are not consciously or unconsciously dependent on their twin for life-giving support. In addition, these twins are not unconsciously or consciously dependent on the bond they share with their twin to support their sense of self, as with the polarized twin bond.

Twins with an individual identity bond were the most common in my sample of 30 pairs of adult twins. Twenty-one sets of twins shared an individual identity, as compared with two sets who shared unit identity, four sets who shared interdependent identity, and three sets who had a split identity.

As a group, these twins have the most potential for growth outside of the twinship because they have received enough early parenting. The parents are attached to their twin as well as to their mother or primary caregiver. Family expectations were high, in that these twins were encouraged to achieve as individuals. In addition, and as important, their parents were not overly involved in encouraging their twin children to identify with twinship.

Although mothers in this group have worked to respond to and develop real differences between their twins and to encourage them to be independent of each other, they still experience separation problems from their twin siblings. From my conversations with adults who shared an individual twin bond, I came to understand that the problems they experienced with separation were focused both consciously and unconsciously on an inability to give up the closeness, comfort, and security of twinship. Because these twins are trusted friends with shared values and dreams, they have difficulty finding other people who find them as compelling as their twin. But these twins are motivated to give up this closeness to pursue adult interests. Because these twins have had positive experiences with a close, intimate relationship, they seek out other close relationships and expect that they will be positive.

In summary, the bond between individual identity twins is based on realistic trust, sharing, and deep concern for each other. These twins are not overly involved with each other, as with interdependent identity twins. In addition, they are not overly involved with their role in the twinship, as is found with split identity twins. Individual identity twins don't need to be copies of, or opposites of, each other. They are content with knowing they share their childhood and adolescent memories. They like spending time with each other and sharing their special understanding of each other, but they function on their own without their twin and are able to develop deep relationships with other people.

Denise and Dorothy, identical twins, describe twinship as a positive experience. Their parents encouraged their differences, which allowed them to became distinctive individuals. Denise explained, "There is a deep sense of attachment in just being together." Dorothy talked about her attachment to her twin: "I am close to Mom and Dad, my kids and husband. I feel like my twin is my closest confidant. I share my secrets and disappointments with her. I miss her when we are apart. We crave our relationship."

Peter and Raymond, fraternal twins, were always encouraged to be independent and unique. They also shared a close bond as children and adolescents. Peter explained, "Our bond is based on trust. It's built on closeness. We understand each other and accept each other's limitations." Raymond added, "I never wished I wasn't a twin."

Charlene and Carrie, identical twins who enjoyed childhood and adolescent twin pranks, were able to develop a strong sense as individuals. They both agree that their bond helps them to never feel alone. It gives them confidence that they understand each other spiritually, emotionally, and mentally. Charlene and Carrie feel blessed that they are twins.

Dede and Diana, identical twins, were raised to be independent. Their mother put a great deal of energy into their individuality. They separated from each other in early adulthood, and they live very different lives. Finding time to be with each other is hard. They agree that "being a twin is all we know. The closeness we had as children is no longer possible because of our busy lives. Now we feel pressure to be together. We hold on to the fantasy that someday we will be closer."

Eileen and Jean, fraternal twins who were separated in adolescence by geographical distance, struggled with redefining their bond as adults. Both held on to the fantasy that being with their sister would make their lives easier and more understandable. Eventually both women realized that they had idealized their twinship. In their 40s they openly faced disappointments with each other's life choices and coping strategies. By age 50 they had renegotiated a more realistic relationship, which included accepting each other's limitations and deciding whether or not to discuss feelings of anger or resentment. Jean reflected on the evolution of her bond with her sister, saying, "Although we have had hard times seeing the truth of how we are very different, I would never give up the type of understanding and closeness that I have experienced by being a twin."

Ron and Alan are identical twins who were not treated as "the twins." Their parents tried to encourage them to be themselves, "regular brothers." They both seriously disliked being stared at by voyeuristic onlookers because of their twinship. They were separated in kindergarten and remained close to each other throughout their years of schooling, while establishing different friends and interests. It was not particularly difficult for Alan and Ron to separate in college. These men have been involved in romantic relationships but have never married.

Ron and Alan value their own individuality and their bond with each other. They are still annoyed by the public attention they receive from casual onlookers, and they avoid appearing in public as the "twin entertainment." They share a deep and intense bond that is easy to access. Their bond is based on shared memories and experiences, and a capacity to quickly relate to the other's state of mind. Ron explained, "It's easy to talk about everything. We can be built-in best friends." Alan expanded on his brother's thoughts. "Sometimes we can just look at each other and we know what the other one is thinking."

Natalie and Veronica were treated as individuals, but the trauma of their childhood experiences kept them close. They established separate lives through marriage and family, but Veronica and Natalie still feel very attached to each other and remain constant companions in their personal and professional lives. They describe their bond as "a deep connection."

Robert and Gary were never treated as a unit. They were brought up as brothers who were very close, but they describe a special intimacy between them that is not shared with their sister or other brothers. Robert explained that their bond was very intense and often did not involve talking to each other. He recalled times spent with his brother on the road where they were just happy to be together, idyllic days that are representative of their connection. Gary describes their special closeness as "confidants to one another" even though they have made different choices for their lives.

Julie and Greg were treated as individuals because of their gender differences. They were very close as children, always playing together and doing their schoolwork together. In adolescence they began to separate from each other when they started to date. Marriage and job demands created more distance between these twins. When asked to describe her bond with her brother, Julie said, "We were very close as children. Now, I feel pressured to be close to Greg because we are twins." Greg expanded on his sister's feelings. "I do not feel like we share a special bond as adults. I feel closer to my father and brother."

These examples of the individual identity bond demonstrate the range and variety of relationships that twins who have successfully separated from their co-twin can share. A greater capacity for individual development is the common thread.

A SUMMARY OF TWINNING BONDS

The pattern of twinship very clearly defined the quality of the bond that twins shared. Unit identity twins' lives were highly interconnected. They shared a symbiotic bond and could not function successfully without each other. Interdependent identity twins were overly invested in their co-twin's daily life experiences. Because they were so narcissistically enmeshed, they accepted each other with a virulent, blind faith that was anathema to other twins. Polar opposite pairs (split identity twins) held on to their childhood identities as the bad twin or the good twin even as adults. However, they were not close to their twin after adolescence because their shared childhood bond became diffused. Individual identity twins successfully separated from each other after adolescence, redeveloping a newer version of their old relationship. They shared a deep bond as adults, taking into consideration each other's strengths and weaknesses. Male-female (boy-girl) twins appeared to long for a special bond because they were twins, but it was not really there. As adults, they have a very strong sibling bond, not an intense twin bond.

In infancy and childhood, twins are very close to each other. They share a deep and profound bond based on parallel development and proper parenting that promotes individuality. In addition, the attention they receive from outsiders who find them curious and abnormal deepens their sense of connection. Eventually young twins come to believe that they are special, even unique, because of all the attention they receive. They have fun with "double trouble" antics and are partners in harmless teasing and deception.

Adolescence serves to diffuse the bond that twins share as they make new, separate friends and explore different interests. The drive for separateness creates competition between twins, which is inevitable. Competition between twins eventually lessens in adulthood, midlife is a time of reconciliation, and old age leads to genuine acceptance and concern. Sara and Ann, 88 years old at the time of the study, herewith share their experiences of twinship, which confirmed my perspective on the changing nature of the twin bond.

Sara and Ann were born in the Midwest in 1912 to a well-to-do family. Their parents were delighted and proud to have fraternal twin daughters to add to their existing family, which consisted of two sons. These girls were treated as equals; one was not favored over the other. Sara, who was more outgoing and social, was closer to her mother. Ann, who was quieter, was closer to her father. Ann and Sara share an individual identity bond because of the quality of parenting they received.

As was traditional when they were growing up, Sara and Ann dressed alike until they graduated from high school. In elementary school they were separated from each other whenever possible. When the girls were in seventh grade, the family moved to California. They recall becoming very dependent on each other at this time because of having to confront a new school and new social situations. By high school they began to develop separate interests and separate friends. Ann went to business school while Sara went to UCLA to study social work. They married within one year of each other. Each of these women had one child and remained married until the death of their spouse.

Sara lived a more extravagant life than her sister. She traveled around the world with her husband and was never forced to support herself. Ann lived a more middle-class life, working in a business with her husband. Ann and Sara accepted each other's different lifestyles. They did not fight or compete with each other as adults. They worked through their differences without feeling as though they had to be copies of each other.

Sara was concerned, when I interviewed her, that her sister was staying home too much and perhaps needed some live-in help. These women did not want to live together. Ann was happy living on her own, as was Sara. The women talk to each other every day. Sara said, "I feel sorry for someone who doesn't have a twin sister." Ann agrees that being a twin has made her life more interesting and lively.

All of the family members who commented about the bond between twins emphasized that it was different from relationships they had observed among non-twins. Because family members are keen observers of their relatives, I felt sure that their observations were accurate, informative, and insightful. Across the board, no matter what pattern of twinship their twin relatives were categorized as, family members agreed that the twin bond was a powerful and special connection. Parents, siblings, cousins, children, grandparents, and spouses all believed that it was an inexplicable dominant force in family life.

Most interestingly, all the family members with whom I spoke were somewhat in awe of the twins in their family. Their initial reaction was similar to distant onlookers who were mesmerized by twins. Relatives of twins appeared on the surface to be proud, amused, and curious about the "look-alikes" in their family. Usually, family members thought beyond the freakish or weird quality of twinship and treated their twin relatives as individuals. In most instances relatives found twins to be entertaining as well as a curiosity, and initially focused on this aspect of their identity. When looking closer at their twin relatives, families were able to see differences and react appropriately, but it definitely required time to get beyond the "oh, it's cute that they are twins" stage.

General reactions were found among sisters and brothers of twins. Most single sisters and brothers initially felt left out of the special bond their twin siblings shared. As the twins were integrated into the family, brothers and sisters formed unique alliances with each twin or with the pair. In some instances, the third child joined the pair and they became a gang. Or one twin and one sibling would form a special alliance, leaving the other twin out to identify with a parent or other sibling. Alliances that were established in childhood lasted into adulthood.

Cousins, aunts, and uncles were more likely to relate to the twins as a pair in childhood. As differences between the twin pair became more obvious, unique relationships were established with these relatives. Twinship was always a cornerstone of these relationships, no matter what alliances were formed later in life.

Husbands or wives openly dealt with the primary bond between "the twins" to establish their own unique relationship. Spouses of interdependent identity twins were careful to respect their "twin-in-law" because of the power of the bond they were competing with for attention and love.

Spouses of split identity twins were confused by the ambivalence these twins had for each other. At one moment their spouse needed closeness, sharing, and companionship. Just as surely and quickly, the spouse detached from her twin because of overwhelming feelings of competition, disappointment, or anger.

Spouses of twins with an individual identity were, more often than not, critical of the other twin's husband or wife. Criticism among individuated twins was tolerated as acceptable. For example, Janet's husband might think that

Naomi's husband was a jerk, but he accepted this and formed an amicable, but somewhat distant, relationship.

Husbands and wives of twins have unique problems to contend with because they always live in the shadow of their partner's early childhood bond. Inevitably, twins consciously or unconsciously want to re-create their twinship with people with whom they are very close. They want to be exquisitely understood as they were in childhood, and they want to develop an intense communication style. Immediate understanding and rapid communication is not always possible, even in the best of adult relationships. Twins face disappointment and have to work through the loss of the comfort of their twin as they become involved in adult relationships.

The children of twins are perhaps the most fortunate onlookers of the twin relationship. They can be delighted and entertained by their aunt's or uncle's gifts and pranks, yet at the same time they establish a primary bond with their own parent that is based on love, attention, and caring. Of course, a boy whose mother is a twin is on the front line when things go wrong between his mother and his aunt, so he can appreciate twinship on a profound level. Melinda's son said, "My mother and my aunt have a deeply troubled relationship. The communication between them is intense and immediate. It is hard to keep up with what is going on between them."

I was fascinated and moved when Ann told me that her children still celebrate her birthday and her deceased sister's birthday together because they know the intensity of her feelings for Arlene.

CONCLUSIONS

Whether or not a precise definition of the twin bond can be established or agreed upon, it exists in the life experiences of twins and their families. The bond between twins is a powerful life force that determines personality characteristics as well as life choices. The bond for all twins is very intense in childhood, but takes on different characteristics as twins grow older and wiser.

Differences between the twin bond and the sibling bond are obvious on a superficial level, but on a deeper level it is difficult to put these differences into words. Siblings who are very close can be similar to twins, but twins can never be just brothers or sisters. Animosity between twins is usually based on a faulty parent-child relationship, whereas animosity between siblings can be attributed to distinctive personalities as well as the quality of parenting. Because of the intensity of the twin bond, twins are more at risk of suffering from mismanaged caregiving than single children are.

6

Twins and Psychotherapy

While reviewing and recording developmental issues and psychological histories with the adult twins who chose to participate in this research project, questions emerged about possible experiences in psychotherapy. The question, "Have you ever seen a psychotherapist or psychiatrist?" was not asked directly. Questions such as, "How did you deal with your anxiety when you were separated from your twin?," "How was it for you to be the unmarried twin?," "How did you deal with your twin's illness?," or "Have you ever been disappointed in relationships?" provoked responses about psychotherapy.

Many of the adult twins in this study spoke with mental health professionals about issues related to growing up as a twin and the aftereffects of being a twin in a non-twin world. Approximately 40% of the sample reported being involved in psychotherapy or psychoanalysis sometime in their lives. Because of the diversity in age, socioeconomic status, and other demographics for this sample it is impossible to make a statistical analysis of twins' mental health problems as compared with singletons' mental health problems. Anecdotally, it appears that twins had a higher incidence of mental health problems than non-twins.

The initial purposes for entering into a therapeutic experience varied from person to person and included the following:

- Unresolved pain and anger at being abused or neglected in childhood
- Relationship issues with a spouse or serious life partner
- Emotional pain related to divorce
- Serious stress related to the twin sister's or brother's chronic or terminal illness
- Bipolar disorder
- Post-traumatic stress disorder
- Bulimia and anorexia

As might be expected, some of the participants in this study were more open about their emotional conflicts and psychotherapeutic experiences than others.

The goals of therapy and the specific technical approach used—cognitive-behavioral, interpersonal, psychodynamic, or psychoanalytic—varied as well. Nonetheless, even with limited, sketchy information, I was able to make some broad generalizations about the purpose and effectiveness of therapy. I was also privileged to hear some of the more intense therapeutic experiences of one adult twin who participated in this study. This case will be presented later in the chapter.

See Table 6.1 for an overview of the reasons twins looked for mental health interventions.

COMMON EXPERIENCES OF TWINS IN PSYCHOTHERAPY

Adult twins spoke openly about their experiences in psychotherapy. I found the following common threads:

Table 6.1
Psychopathology across Twin Bonds

Pattern of Twinship	Psychological Problems	Type of Psychotherapy
Unit Identity	Clinical depression	None
	Post-traumatic stress disorder	
Interdependent Identity	Clinical depression	Crisis intervention
	Suicide	Long-term psychodynamic psychotherapy
Split Identity	Clinical depression	Long-term psychodynamic psychotherapy
	Post-traumatic stress disorder	
	Eating disorders	
Individual Identity	Anxiety disorders	Short- or long-term psychodynamic psychotherapy
	Bipolar disorder	
	Adjustment disorders	

1. Twins enjoyed insight into themselves and their twinship, so psychotherapy was highly successful for the twins who sought out and found a therapist to work with on their emotional issues.

2. Adult twins enjoyed therapy because their childhood experiences, which were highly interactional, led them to expect they could have someone to talk to who would pay attention and give them feedback about themselves.

3. The therapist became a twin substitute on a conscious and unconscious level.

4. Psychotherapy and psychoanalysis were replacements for those with dysfunctional twin interactions. In these situations psychotherapy was a corrective emotional experience.

5. Psychotherapy that did not account for twin developmental needs and issues was not useful. In other words, the idiosyncrasies of twinship had to be taken into account in the therapeutic approach or the client would not make a commitment to therapy.

6. Treatment failure had a variety of consequences for twins. One twin committed suicide, and other twins had seriously unfortunate experiences.

7. Twins are used to and need more feedback from therapy. Therapists who were active in sessions were more effective than therapists who took a passive or mostly silent approach.

8. The therapist's capacity to accept the central role of twinship in all emotional and situational problems was imperative if concrete and lasting psychological growth was to be accomplished.

9. Relating to a twin as a member of a twin pair rather than as a single person was essential. For example, the therapist needed to realize that the patient had a real need for connectedness and identification with the therapist. When twins saw therapists who were also twins, this goal was easier to accomplish. Non-twin therapists needed to work hard at understanding twin issues.

10. Psychotherapy should have a realistic goal based on the personality structure of the twin client. For example, a twin with an interdependent identity had difficulty establishing firm psychological boundaries with his co-twin. The therapist may need to provide some insight on how he can set limits with his sibling, without expecting him to form a totally distinct sense of self.

11. Issues of twin loss and twin bereavement were oftentimes very ethereal, and required a capacity for openness and spirituality on the part of the therapist.

12. Allowing a twin sister or brother to participate with the client, if necessary, was extremely helpful and lent a depth of understanding to the therapist.

CHILDHOOD NEGLECT AND ABUSE

Nine out of 30 sets of adult twins received very marginal parenting, which is a serious form of childhood abuse or neglect. The two sets of unit identity twins, the four sets of interdependent identity twins, and the three sets of split identity twins were all victims of serious pervasive parental abuse and neglect because they failed to receive adequate attention to their individual differences. Some of these sets of twins were physically and sexually abused as well. The bond that all these twins shared in childhood was parentified; simply stated, when twins do not get enough individual attention from their parents, they serve as parent figures to each other. This early primary dependency on each other had serious, long-standing, and tenacious repercussions for their personality development.

Unit identity twins did not seek the empathy of psychotherapy because they were each other's exclusive advisers. They did not have the capacity or inclination to resolve psychic injuries related to childhood abuse, neglect, and trauma.

Interdependent identity twins did not enter therapy because they were troubled by their childhood experiences. Instead, their therapeutic concern was some danger to their co-twin's well-being, such as serious illness, clinical depression, or suicidal ideation. When interdependent identity twins entered therapy, they were later able to confront serious childhood abuse and neglect.

Split identity twins realized that they had troubled relationships with their parents because of the florid use of projection by all family members. At some point in adolescence they were consciously aware that one of them was less favored than the other for no apparent reason. As children they were unconsciously or subconsciously aware of this distinction. The devalued twin sought out therapy to overcome shame and confusion related to being mistreated, that is, being humiliated and abused, and being taken advantage of by the family. The idealized twin suffered as well, because she had an inflated sense of entitlement and serious confusion about realistic expectations for others. The idealized twin was less likely to be in need of therapy than her devalued sister.

Mistreatment and abuse was reported by twins with an individualized identity as well. However, in these instances, resolution of emotional pain related to cruel and overbearing behavior by parental figures left less drastic characterological scars. The less pervasive the parental abuse and neglect, the easier it was for twins to deal with and overcome the painful side effects of depression, shame, humiliation, and poor self-esteem.

THERAPEUTIC INTERVENTIONS FOR VICTIMS OF CHILDHOOD ABUSE

Interdependent Identity

Ann and Arlene, interdependent identity twins, consulted a clinical social worker for issues related to childhood abuse and neglect when they were 20 years old. The clinical issue that was explored was a manifestation of childhood abuse: intense separation anxiety. Ann and Arlene had extreme difficulty tolerating a period of necessary separation from each other (because of work commitments). Unfortunately, the therapist they consulted did not understand the intensity of the separation problem and performed what was described to me as "role-changing" therapy, or a type of interactional analysis. Each of the twins was asked to pretend that they were the other twin while sitting in different chairs in the therapist's office, an absurd simplification of their problem that forced Ann and Arlene to abruptly terminate therapy. They did not begin to work at their issues of overreliance on each other, and instead began to act out their anxieties in order to contain them. Ann and Arlene each married the first man who asked her and who also seemed marginally stable, in order to have a dependable in-house twin substitute. Ann had children to replace the emptiness she felt from not being in continuous contact with Arlene. For many years these young women pretended they were coping with their separation anxiety from each other.

At age 26, Arlene consulted a psychiatrist for eight months to resolve clinical depression and suicidal ideation that stemmed from her divorce and the great geographical distance from her twin sister. The psychiatrist did not understand the intensity of Arlene's problems with tolerating separation from her sister in times of stress. Arlene's therapeutic encounter was highly ineffective; she became more and more despondent and hopeless. Her psychiatrist did not understand how profoundly depressed she really was, or Arlene did not communicate her feelings well. She committed suicide by running her car's engine in an enclosed garage. The psychiatrist was shocked at this outcome, and her sister was in a state of disbelief. Ann never thought her sister would do something so drastic.

Ann and the family contacted the psychiatrist after the funeral and determined that he had not been aware of Arlene's determination to take her life. A lawsuit was filed against this psychiatrist for wrongful death, and as part of this process Ann and her family reviewed the treatment records, which indicated that Arlene was drinking six to eight glasses of wine a day. In psychotherapy Arlene and the psychiatrist had been working on understanding the effects of parental hostility and rejection because of her mother's alcoholism. Arlene herself had become an alcoholic and was afraid to admit this to her family, carefully planning every conversation so that no one would suspect her problem.

This lawsuit was dropped because of insufficient evidence against the doctor, but many questions remain unanswered. Was Arlene's addiction a way of separating from her twin sister? Would a deeper understanding of the differences in development between twins and single children have helped prevent this suicide? Although as a psychologist I dislike second-guessing, I believe a deeper understanding of twinship would have helped.

Because of her sister's abject treatment failure, concluding with Arlene's death, Ann realized that she had to take seriously the abuse and neglect in her childhood. It took Ann 10 years to build up her confidence so that she might trust someone to understand the pain of her childhood and the loss of her sister. Fortunately, she found a psychologist who was a twin to help her sort out her traumatic experiences. With intensive psychoanalytic psychotherapy

Ann was able to grieve over the loss of her sister and make a better life for herself and her family.

Split Identity

All three sets of split identity twins sought out the support of psychotherapy or psychoanalysis as young adults. These twins realized that they had been seriously abused as children. Mary and Melinda, Emily and Deena, and Cindy and Debbie all suffered from clinical depression, resultant poor self-esteem, and a lack of clear goals for their lives. They all worked in psychoanalysis or psychotherapy to process the pain of their childhood in the hope of recovering from long-standing depression. Intensive psychotherapy helped these women reinvent themselves.

Emily and Deena both entered psychoanalysis as young adults. Emily, who was treated as the bad or devalued twin, suffered from clinical depression when she first sought out support and insight into herself. She was married and had two children, but she always felt unhappy with herself. Her doctor helped her understand her role in the family, and she learned to stand up to Deena and follow her own interests and inclinations. Emily dealt with disappointment with her husband, who was close to her but very different from her twin sister. She became aware of her tendency to try to develop close relationships with other people, and gradually she separated from her twin and began to feel more comfortable with herself. This therapeutic encounter was considered successful when Emily started studying to be an actress.

Deena, the valued or idealized twin, married at the same time as Emily and had four children. Deena's husband was a wealthy and prominent doctor, who provided a great deal of financial comfort for his family. Unfortunately, Deena began to suffer from a serious depression when her mother died. Deena was a fragile, high-strung person who needed continual emotional support. Growing up, she had always been supported by Emily, who put Deena's need for attention in front of her own needs. However, as Emily got stronger, Deena began to feel more needy and deprived of attention, so she entered into intensive psychoanalysis, which provided her with much needed support. With her doctor's help, she gradually dealt with her extreme neediness and dependency issues, and learned to control her feelings by understanding that she did not always need to be the center of attention or the most important person in the room. She was able to form new close attachments and be attentive to her children and husband, who in turn felt very close to her.

Understandably but unfortunately, she could not deal with her sister's need for autonomy. Deena and Emily began to disagree in their mid-20s, and could never again seem to agree. A great deal of energy was put into mending their adult relationship, to no avail. Deena could not tolerate Emily's success and Emily could not abide Deena's criticism.

Emily moved away from her sister in midlife to pursue her acting career. Leaving her sister and her hometown to start a new life precipitated an agitated depression, and she consulted a psychiatrist when she had suicidal thoughts. Once again she entered psychoanalysis. This treatment intervention helped Emily pursue her dream of becoming an actress as well as deal with her disappointment with Deena and her sister's role as the good one in the family.

Emily and Deena were never able to resolve their anger with each other nor to reconnect as adults in spite of decades of psychotherapy. Emily is still very conflicted about being a twin. Although she loves and respects her sister, she believes strongly that twinship is a curse.

Mary and Melinda also sought out psychoanalysis to deal with the labels they were assigned as children and with the emotional scars that created problems for them as adults. As a young woman, Melinda always felt inadequate, suffering from a clinical depression related to poor self-esteem. She worked with a psychoanalyst to understand the antecedents of her depression. To conquer her poor self-esteem she found new ways to express herself that allowed her to take in positive feedback from others and from her own achievements. In addition, Melinda dealt with her deep-seated anger at Mary and realized that it was better for her to keep her distance from Mary. Psychoanalysis helped Melinda to separate from her twin sister and her "bad twin" self-image.

Mary sought out psychotherapy in times of crisis with her children or with her husband. In the interview for this book, Mary was not especially open about the therapeutic process she involved herself in. In spite of Mary's guardedness, it became clear that psychotherapy helped her separate from Melinda's problems, and Mary became aware that she felt burdened by being a twin as an adult. She felt ashamed of Melinda and ashamed of herself when she was with Melinda. The fond memories of her childhood twinship were unattainable in adulthood. Mary did not want to reconnect with Melinda, whom she experienced as critical of her. In addition, Mary was ashamed of Melinda whenever she did not feel threatened by her or feel less than her. After therapy Mary seemed to enjoy her freedom from being a twin.

Mary and Melinda came to understand, through years of separate psychoanalytic experiences, how their twinship had created a wedge between them. In midlife they became tired of trying to resolve their differences of opinion, so now they live separate lives. The memories of the abuse of their childhood are painfully evoked when they are together, which makes it difficult for them to see each other.

In the interview for this book, Cindy and Debbie were not open about their experiences in psychotherapy. What can be assumed is that both of these women saw psychotherapists to explore issues that focused on poor self-esteem and depression related to their childhood and to their twinship.

Dealing with abusive experiences in psychotherapy or psychoanalysis allowed all three sets of women to think about what they wanted for themselves, separate from family expectations and twin sister expectations. As these women gained insight into how they were labeled and mistreated, they were able to see themselves in a more accurate light, and they were encouraged to pursue their own interests and dreams for the future.

Emily became a successful actress, whereas Deena allowed herself to be a homemaker for her husband and children. Cindy moved far away from home and raised a family. Debbie stayed close to home, ran a business, and raised a daughter. Mary broadened her academic focus and raised a family. Melinda married, had two children, and completed graduate school.

Individual Identity

Dede and Diana were raised by a psychologically minded mother to seek out their own identities. As adolescents they had to deal with their father's manic-depressive illness. In spite of extensive medical and psychiatric intervention, he would become agitated, abusive, or out of control, or retreat into depression. His instability contributed to Dede and Diana's insecurity with men. As young adults these twins each sought out the help of psychoanalysis to overcome their issues with men and their fears of commitment. Psychoanalysis helped each of these women to eventually resolve their anger at their father and to marry and have several children.

Arnold and Cynthia were also neglected and emotionally abused as children. By the age of 20 both of their parents had died. These twins did not turn to each other to deal with issues of depression, rage, and poor self-esteem. Instead, Cynthia and Arnold turned to mental health professionals for support and insight into their childhood.

Cynthia saw a female psychotherapist for five years to develop problem-solving strategies and to gain support and insight into her self-loathing and self-defeating behavior. She eventually graduated from college and married, with the help of her therapist.

Arnold had an enormous amount of unresolved anger at his parents for providing an emotionally and financially unstable childhood. He saw a series of psychotherapists who helped channel his rage into productive behavior. Arnold returned to college and became a highly successful businessman, fathering two children with his first wife and another child with his second wife. Other marriages did not lead to more children for Arnold.

RELATIONSHIP ISSUES WITH A SPOUSE OR OTHER ROMANTIC PARTNER

All of the twins who sought out psychotherapy or psychoanalysis had relationship issues with their partner, which were usually based on an unresolved idealization of twinship. In other words, twins thought they should receive the same kind of exquisite attention from their romantic partner as they did from their twin. Of course, this was an almost impossible expectation to meet, so twins were often disappointed. Twins' longings for attention and understanding made it difficult for new significant others to live up to their "twin partner" fantasies.

Talking with one's twin about a relationship issue concerning a husband, wife, or lover had limited value, because the formation of a new attachment was a way of separating from the twin. Or twins were clearly too close for comfort to give advice or support on their replacement.

Twins turned to psychotherapists for help in understanding their frustrations with non-twin relationships. In many cases, this frustration was a reflection of anxiety in separating from their twin sibling. Therapy that was successful focused on helping the twin verbalize precisely what he was concerned with and really wanted from his new partner. Oftentimes, including the spouse was important in these interventions.

Therapeutic Interventions

Understanding the limits of intimacy in adult relationships was a common problem that twins wanted to address in psychotherapy. Dealing with separation anxiety from the twin sibling was a key element in resolving this problem. Once an adult twin could admit that she had a problem understanding what to expect from others in adult relationships, the process of establishing new and less demanding expectations for others was not so formidable.

The potential pitfalls of being a twin in a non-twin world were often difficult for psychotherapists or psychoanalysts to understand. The twin patient easily felt misunderstood by significant others who were not as close as her co-twin. In addition, expectations for the new twin substitute were extremely unrealistic. Whatever approach the therapist used to help her patient come to terms with the limits of adult intimacy, the goals were similar. Twin patients with this psychological problem—an overdetermined need for intimacy—were encouraged to understand the roots of their problem and to redirect their passion for intimacy into developing a career, business, or family.

It was a difficult therapeutic process to actually work through a twin patient's need for exquisite intimacy. Although it was clear that refocusing psychic energy on career, education, family, or other new interest provided symptom relief (from the absence of the understanding nature of twinship), it required more effort to help twins establish realistic expectations for being with others. Oftentimes the therapist had to define clear limits for those twins who wanted to merge with or be totally understood by their therapist.

Successful resolution, through psychotherapy or psychoanalysis, of the deep emotional issues of being a twin in a non-twin world was dependent on the capacity of the therapist or analyst to tune in to the patient's pain of losing the extreme closeness of her early twin attachment.

Janet and Naomi, individual identity twins, went to separate colleges. Janet met her future husband while she was involved in her graduate education. She had a great deal of difficulty accepting the emotional limitations of her romantic relationship, and began psychoanalysis to understand her reservations about marriage. Eventually Janet married after refining her expectations about non-twin relationships. Naomi sought out less intensive therapy because she married a professor who could not afford an expensive analyst.

EMOTIONAL PAIN RELATED TO DIVORCE

Many of the twins who participated in this study married and then divorced. What was extremely interesting about this particular issue was that twins in the process of divorce sought out the support and advice of a psychotherapist rather than their co-twin. Divorced twins did not want to ask their twin sibling for emotional help for two primary reasons. First, they felt that their co-twin could not understand what they were going through. Second, there was a great deal of shame related to divorce, so twins thought that they had made a serious mistake and that their co-twin would be critical of them. This fear was usually unfounded, because in many instances twin brothers or sisters provided an open door for comfort and nurturing.

In contrast, from my experience working as a psychotherapist, it is common for brothers and sisters to turn to each other for comfort and support when they are in the process of divorce. Singletons with whom I have worked do not have as much of a sense of failure about the breakup of a relationship. Even though divorce is an emotional issue for everyone involved, twins seem to be much more vulnerable to despair about the loss of a relationship than sisters and brothers. In my experience, brothers and sisters think more about property issues, financial settlement, and child custody.

Therapeutic Interventions

Twins sought out supportive therapy to understand the relationship problems that could not be worked through in their marriages. In addition, they looked for advice and understanding in new relationships, usually resulting in a brief therapeutic encounter.

Dorothy married three months after Denise. Her marriage was very much for appearance's sake; she did not have a deep relationship with her husband. When the marriage split up because of incompatibility, Dorothy talked to a female psychologist instead of to her sister.

Peter married five months before his brother Raymond, but both men were divorced within two years. Neither twin spoke with his brother about the divorce. Rather, they spoke with marriage counselors and social workers to get a better understanding of how to function in a non-twin relationship. Peter and Raymond both remarried and have successfully stayed that way.

Mary divorced her first husband after five years of marriage. She consulted a marriage and family counselor instead of talking with Melinda. In therapy she realized that she wanted to have a family and a more stable life like her sister.

STRESS RELATED TO A TWIN'S SERIOUS OR TERMINAL ILLNESS

Many of the twins in this study had to deal with serious illness. Some twins were overwhelmed by the prospect of losing their twin, and they sought out psychotherapy to process the effects of the illness and their looming potential loss.

Therapeutic Interventions

Therapeutic interventions involved stress management and brief psychodynamic psychotherapy. Usually these interventions were very brief.

Candy and Serena survived Candy's thyroid cancer without therapeutic intervention. When Serena's potentially life-threatening cancer was diagnosed, Candy went to see a therapist for the first time in her life. With five sessions of therapy Candy learned to accept, on an intellectual level, that Serena had made different choices in her life regarding her health and well-being. Understanding that she was not responsible for Serena's illness was the goal of this treatment.

BIPOLAR DISORDER

Charlene and Carrie's bipolar disorder was diagnosed in their early 20s. These women had received enough individual attention as young children from their parents to establish an individual identity twin bond. Their childhood was typical of twins who are capable of separating from each other and establishing distinctive interests and friends.

As is common with bipolar disorder, evidence of mood swings was apparent in adolescence. Charlene and Carrie were often impulsive, and they acted out their anger or irritability by becoming gang members. Both suffered from bouts of sadness and depression as teenagers. The more out-of-control symptoms were apparent when they went to separate colleges. Charlene became seriously depressed and used Carrie to help her through her pain. Charlene did not attempt suicide because Carrie was there for her. When Carrie started to suffer from a very serious depression in her early 20s, these twins sought out separate therapists to understand their emotional instability.

Therapeutic Interventions

Carrie and Charlene were involved in family counseling as teenagers to help them express their anger and frustrations. Their mother was quite concerned

about their connections with gang members. Carrie also had difficulty achiev-
ing in school. This therapeutic experience in family therapy seemed to calm
these twins down, and they were able to graduate from high school and attend
separate colleges.

As young adults it became apparent to both of them that they suffered from
serious mood swings. They would become manic or depressed easily. These
cycles of mania and depression alternated between the twins, so they were
rarely out of control at the same time, which was terrifying when it occurred.
Charlene and Carrie sought out different therapists to deal with their mood
swings. They always wanted a backup to control their moodiness.

Carrie was more active in confronting this mental illness. She chose to work
with a psychiatrist who prescribed different types of psychotropic medications.
Carrie also worked with the psychiatrist to understand the stressful situations
that triggered her mood swings. In psychotherapy she became more aware of
issues related to her twinship and how these issues affected her bipolar disorder.
Through psychotherapy Carrie realized that she longed to be independent, and
on her own: an individual, not a twin. Carrie also learned it was crucial to turn
to Charlene and to her family when she was in trouble, and her twin sister
became an essential support system.

Charlene took a less conventional approach to treating her bipolar disorder.
She was not as concerned with her individuality as Carrie. Charlene began
psychodynamic psychotherapy to understand her relationships with family
members, and she worked on getting her life into a more stable state. With
her therapist she identified particular types of people and places that made her
feel pressured, using stress management techniques to understand what triggered her moodiness. She did not take any psychotropic medications, instead
relying on herbal remedies to control her mood swings. Charlene is comfortable
turning to her sister and her family for help.

Charlene and Carrie are not in psychotherapy together. They like to keep
their relationships with their therapists separate from their twinship. However,
they are aware of their moods and help each other when they feel concerned
that a serious episode of mania or depression could ensue. This reliance on each
other was not always possible. Carrie lived on the streets as an indigent during
one bout of depression.

POST-TRAUMATIC STRESS DISORDER (PTSD)

One adult twin reported suffering from PTSD, which was a direct outcome
of being sexually molested as a child.

In childhood, adolescence, and young adulthood, Melinda's symptoms of
PTSD were masked by specific phobias, generalized anxiety, and a tendency
toward negative mood swings. This is not an unusual presentation for post-
traumatic stress disorder (Courtois, 1988; Schave, 1993).

The actual physical memories of sexual abuse surfaced in midlife for Melinda after a seriously traumatic loss. This type of recovery of repressed memories is very common (Bass & Davis, 1988; Frederickson, 1992). Melinda worked on recovering these frightening memories of incest in psychoanalysis. Melinda turned to Mary for help in recalling the details of the events that haunted her. Mary was quite concerned for Melinda, and these adult twins reconciled. Together they tried to piece together their shared childhood memories.

Mary wrote Melinda a letter of conciliation, which is excerpted here, after the twins had not spoken for almost 20 years.

Dear Melinda,

Why could I not accept my discomfort? Of course it was hard to accept my shame. Whether it was the shame of the incest or just the shame I felt that goes along with being a twin, which made me feel like I did not have control over my life.

I guess I had enough of seeing you suffer. I simply decided to live in the here and now and take your side, since I was already on your side. I guess I decided to stop fighting with myself and accept our twinship.

Finally, I could listen to what had happened to you and not feel as intensely involved in it as you were. So I could objectify your pain, which had always been my pain. Then we could work together to get beyond the feelings of shame, the feelings of self-hatred, double self-hatred for who I was as an individual and for who I was as your twin sister.

Love, Mary

Mary did help Melinda remember some details of her incestuous experiences. Mary began to question whether she might have been sexually abused as well. Unfortunately, the connection between Mary and Melinda deteriorated once again when new stresses confronted Mary's world and well-being.

Melinda believes the difficulties she and her sister still face when they are together is rooted in their abusive childhood. When she and Mary get together, she is continually reminded that she is the bad one and cannot help being demanding and childish. Memories of the past overwhelm and frighten them, and they move away from each other to ease the pain.

Therapeutic Intervention

Melinda entered psychoanalysis to help her deal with frightening feelings from her childhood that were manifested as PTSD. For many years Melinda worked on getting in touch with her own buried feelings by taking her present-day feelings seriously.

The issue of her twinship and of being the bad twin was delved into deeply. She came to believe that she was molested because she was the bad twin daughter, that the two were one and the same thing. Realizing that she deserved to be treated with respect led her to express deep-seated anger and disappointment with her family.

Changing her status in her family of origin from victim to survivor helped Melinda feel stronger about herself and what she felt entitled to from others. Melinda learned to listen to herself and follow her instincts. When trouble arose again in her relationship with Mary, she was able to tolerate her anxiety, shame, and depression with more equanimity.

BULIMIA AND ANOREXIA

Bulimia and anorexia, eating disorders that are commonly found in adolescence and young adults, were also prevalent with some of the twins who participated in this study. Establishing a sense of identity by trying to maintain a certain weight and body type was more common with adolescent and young adult twins. In many situations eating disorders continued throughout the lives of the women with whom I spoke, who used their weight to hold on to their sense of self. Twins with an interdependent identity bond and split identity bond had episodes of anorexia or bulimia. They did not seek out psychotherapy to deal with these issues directly; rather, eating disorders were dealt with as a function of serious separation anxiety relating to twinship.

Therapeutic Interventions

The twins in this study with anorexia or bulimia sought out psychodynamic psychotherapy. They were not involved in any specific treatment modality for eating disorders. Most interestingly and in stark contrast, many of the non-twins with whom I have had contact sought out psychological treatment or psychotherapy that directly dealt with their eating disorder. For example, these people sought out mental health professionals who specialized in anorexia and bulimia as well as going to group programs such as Overeaters Anonymous.

CASE HISTORY OF A TWIN IN INTENSIVE PSYCHOTHERAPY

Ann suffered alone with the loss of her sister Arlene for more than 10 years. Ann held on to her belief about her sister's motivation in committing suicide. She still believes that "Arlene only wanted to be dead a week or two. She really didn't want to do this. Arlene was not thinking clearly. She thought that her actions were not as permanent as they turned out to be." These beliefs remained in Ann's mind immediately after she learned about her sister's death, throughout her sister's funeral, and in the years she spent raising her four children.

Ann felt that she had no one to turn to who could understand her pain. Her husband, father, stepmother, and brother needed her to be strong and to survive. Even at the funeral when she felt like she did not even have enough strength to breathe, she was strong and silent. She felt as though a cannon had been shot through her chest and shattered parts of her heart. In her deepest moments of grief her family wanted her to appear normal. They wanted her to fill in the gap that was created by her sister's death.

When I met Ann, I was working on a project about twin loss with a research assistant. Ann's sister-in-law had told her about our study, and she volunteered to be in it. Ann was finally ready to talk about the loss of her twin sister. I was astounded by the story of her sister's suicide and Ann's strong but silent reaction. I felt concerned that she had worked too hard on keeping her feelings to herself, and I sensed that she needed to share her pain. In the process of working on the research project, I suggested that she look for a therapist to work with her on her unexplored feelings of grief. I gave her the name of three psychotherapists who I thought might be able to help her. I shared with her that I was also a therapist and a twin, and I offered to work with her as well.

I was surprised when Ann called me to schedule an appointment, because she had remained silent about her grief for so many years. Fortunately, she had found the questions I asked her very thoughtful. She wanted to talk to me because I seemed to understand her sadness and because I too was a twin. Ann did not want to see a therapist who was not a twin, after Arlene's bad experience with the psychiatrist who failed to prevent her suicide. I accepted Ann's reasoning about selecting me as a therapist and suggested that we work together on her problem in extended sessions twice a week. We immediately began working on the feelings that she had kept to herself.

In the beginning of our work I asked Ann to try to imagine what her life would be like if her sister were still with her. What would she say to her sister if she could talk to her now? How would her own life be different if Arlene had lived? These questions helped Ann focus on her profound sense of loss. My capacity to understand the depth of her feelings through questions like these began the healing process of psychotherapy.

Ann related to me the story of her childhood, which has been outlined in previous chapters. As I developed a sense of the dynamics between herself and her sister, I was able to understand how deep the division between Arlene, the social twin, and Ann, the serious twin, really was. Because I comprehended the psychological differences between Ann and her sister, Ann regarded me as someone who would accept her as a single and separate person.

In our initial conversations Ann shared her perception that her husband and family did not want to hear about her pain and that no one could really understand her pain. She said she was relieved that I had noticed she was not in a state of normalcy when I first talked to her. Ann told me that she experienced the emotional loss of her sister the day therapy started. The process of sharing with me her feelings and thoughts about losing her sister built a deep trust between us. Gradually Ann was able to talk about the shame she felt when she told others that her sister had killed herself. She realized she felt that if her sister had really loved her she would not have given up her life. Ann thought that others might see her as unworthy and unlovable. She never imagined that other people could understand that her sister's suicide was not her fault, but to her surprise and relief, people with whom she talked about her loss showed great compassion.

Gradually in therapy Ann understood that her sister's actions were not a reflection of Ann's perceived inadequacy as a twin sister. She began to see herself as a separate person who was entitled to all the rights of single people. Ann started standing up to her husband and asking for what she wanted and needed. To use her words, she "stopped being a wimp." The next critical issue in therapy included rebuilding stronger and more substantial relationships between Ann and her husband, father, and stepmother. This was not a linear process; rather, building in more support for Ann besides her children meant uncovering buried feelings about her sister and her childhood, talking about her feelings, and working to put them into perspective.

Ann recalled that after her sister's suicide her family had expected her to fill in the hole created by the loss of her sister. Since Ann and Arlene had not been treated as separate people, her father, stepmother, and brother expected that she could make up the difference, and Ann came to realize how difficult it was to make up for her sister's absence. She became aware of how much she really missed her sister and what an effort it was to get through every day without her. She realized that she had retreated into being the perfect mother and submissive wife to assuage her guilt for somehow not preventing her sister's death. As we worked together to imagine the motives for her sister's death, Ann realized that it was not her responsibility to prevent her sister's impulsive actions. As Ann began to feel entitled to have her life, she shared with me that she deserved to live and that her sister should have felt likewise. This way of talking about her own life after her sister was gone helped to alleviate any survivor guilt she might have felt.

Another crucial issue in therapy was the role she played as a twin and how this affected her present-day relationships. I came to understand that Ann was the strong twin relative to her sister, the twin you could count on to be as steady as a rock. As a child, Ann was clearly the burdened twin, and as an adult she took on impossible burdens as well. As we worked on establishing realistic goals for Ann in relationship to her husband, children, and parents, she began to feel more lighthearted. She told me that after she left my office, she thought about all the things we had discussed, and felt like she could see things she had never seen before. She saw therapy as an emotionally enlightening process and accepted that she could not get through her grief alone.

Ann and I worked through the anger and alienation that she felt toward her father and stepmother for having totally unrealistic expectations about her capacity to get over Arlene's death. Ann spoke about her anger with her husband for not providing her with emotional support when she needed it most. She accepted responsibility for listening to other people's demands, and she started to say no to her husband and parents when they made unrealistic demands on her. For example, Ann spoke openly about her sadness to her father and husband, even though they thought she had voiced her emotional pain more than adequately. Standing up for her own feelings helped Ann feel alive.

In the therapeutic alliance I became Ann's new twin sister, who knew how she was feeling and what she was thinking. Ann finally had found someone who was attempting to understand her pain and to help her be herself. After working in this therapeutic stance for more than three years, Ann felt like she was entitled to stand up for what she wanted. She divorced her critical, unresponsive husband and opened her own business. She is highly successful in her work and as a parent.

Ann overcame many obstacles in therapy. First, she faced the emotional reality of her twin sister's suicide. Next, she was able to get beyond feeling that she should have prevented her sister's impulsive behavior. Ann realized that her sister did not want to live and that in no way could she have been more loving and worthy or able to save her sister's life. Finally, Ann stood up for her feelings and ideas and became the person she wanted to be.

Some unfinished therapy related to Ann's decision to avoid intense romantic relationships. For many years she has felt that her children have replaced her sister's companionship and love. On a deep level she is afraid to remarry, as it might be a betrayal of the bond she shares with her deceased sister.

CONCLUSIONS

Many of the adult twins in this study sought out the insight and support of psychotherapy or psychoanalysis to deal with issues related to twinship, new non-twin relationships, child abuse, PTSD, bipolar disorder, and bereavement.

To make progress in psychotherapy, adult twins needed to find a therapist who understood twin developmental issues, and who was able to form an active and deep therapeutic alliance with their patient. Twins have an intense need to be understood and to be mirrored by their therapist, and they did better in therapeutic relationships that involved high levels of attentiveness. Many of the individuals who participated in this study were not helped by the psychotherapeutic process. These treatment failures were related to the therapist's inability to understand the primary nature of the twinning bond. The other individuals who entered therapy gained insight into their twinship, which helped them to relate more honestly to their twin and to significant others in their lives.

Specifically, twins who sought out psychotherapy reported at first being very skeptical about taking intimate advice from another person who was not their twin, but who functioned in a twinlike role rather than as a friend or romantic partner. The twins in this sample who sought out therapy and continued in therapy came to trust their therapist and were able to deal with their anger and disappointment with their co-twin. Oftentimes therapy created tension between twins. The therapists who were effective needed to have a special attentiveness to the closeness that twins share, while at the same time fostering separation between the pair.

Working with twins in psychotherapy is very difficult and challenging compared with working with individuals who have sisters and brothers. These difficulties and complexities are related to the deep transferences and resistances—expectations and disappointments—that twins experience with their therapist.

7

Genetic Endowment and the Environment

NATURE VERSUS NURTURE IN THE 21ST CENTURY

Using identical and fraternal twins as subjects, volumes of scientific articles have been written on the relative importance of genetic influences compared with the effect of environmental stimulation and stress upon the individual (Cohen et al., 1977; Gessell, 1941; Jensen, 1969; Matheny, 1980; Mittler, 1971; Newman, Freeman & Holzinger, 1937; Segal, 1999; Shields, 1962). In essence, this research suggests that on measurable aspects of personality, such as intelligence, introversion, or sociability, identical twins are more genetically similar than fraternal twins or single siblings. In addition, behavioral genetic studies have shown that identical twins are more similar than fraternal twins or single siblings when it comes to susceptibility to the disease process. If one identical twin gets a diagnosis of cancer, heart disease, or mental illness, such as schizophrenia, bipolar disorder, depression, or panic disorder, the other identical twin is much more likely to suffer from these diseases than the single sibling or fraternal twin.

Genetic studies have proven that physical characteristics, such as eye and hair color or height and weight, are inherited. Twins are walking proof of the importance of genetic determinants of identity. Perhaps this is why people are mesmerized when they see twins together, looking for all the world like copies of each other. It reminds us that some aspects of life are given and cannot be changed.

Recently, twin studies have been used to determine the genetic aspect of homosexuality (Bailey & Pillard, 1991; King & McDonald, 1992). These studies ponder the question, "Do all identical twins have the same sexual orientation?" There were no stated conclusions from this research, but it was suggested that there is some genetic contribution to sexual orientation. This research challenges previous psychoanalytic theory, which suggests that homosexuality is determined in part by maternal influences, attitudes, and needs (Stoller, 1968).

It might be easy to believe that genetics dominates human development, but the importance of the environment is not ruled out, even by geneticists.

Environment can and does affect the genetic endowment. Indeed, there is a great deal of serious interest and research on how important the optimal environment is to health and longevity. Can we overcome our genetic underpinnings through nutrition, diet, exercise, stress management, and education? The answer is yes. The nature versus nurture controversy has taken on new life in the 21st century.

Psychoanalytic and psychodynamic research using twins as subjects was ahead of its time because it looked at the importance of interpersonal interaction as a part of environment. Such research adds a new dimension to understanding child and adult development, because it considers the effect of parent-child interaction on intra-psychic growth and development (Burlingham, 1952; Dibble & Cohen, 1981; Gifford et al., 1966; Leonard, 1961; Lytton, 1980; Schave, 1982; Zazzo, 1960). In addition, developmental psychologists accept the genetic blueprint as a distinct, unchangeable part of child development.

By accepting the importance of the parent-child interaction as fundamental to the growth and development of personality, environment includes the intra-psychic interaction between the mother and child (Bell, 1977; Bowlby, 1958; Erickson, 1950; Lytton, Conway & Suave, 1977; Mahler, 1967; Sullivan, 1953).

Contemporary twin research studies provide insight into the importance of intra-psychic phenomena and the importance of the mother-child interaction and the inter-twin relationship. This research suggests that the environment of the mother and child is crucial to growth and well-being. Twinship is affected by parenting and can replace aspects of parenting in troubled home environments, but twinship alone is not enough to complete the cycle of development. Maternal interaction is the crucial environmental factor in development (Schave & Ciriello, 1983).

MOTHER-CHILD INTERACTION: THE CRUCIAL DETERMINANT OF EARLY DEVELOPMENT

The impossibility of ruling out genetic determinants is understandable. Also, environment is a continuous determinant of who we become as we grow up. My current research on twin development underscores that the most important aspect of the environment is the mother-child bond. Socioeconomic status, health care, and education can in no way make up for deficiencies or damage caused by inadequate or terribly limited parenting. The mother's capacity to be attentive to her child's unique developmental needs is what melds the genetic endowment and environmental influences.

In twin development, it is the mother's psychological mindedness and the capacity to differentiate between her twin children that determines the overall psychological well-being of her children later in life. Although it may at first be easier for a mother of fraternal twins to see differences between her children and to know that her twins are not genetically identical, over time mothers of identical and fraternal twins face the same problem of relating to each twin child as a distinct individual.

CHALLENGING THE GENETIC HYPOTHESIS

The purpose of my research was not focused on the role of genetic endowment in human development; however, some interesting findings came to light when interviewing the adult twins in this study, which clarify the importance of the environment, especially parenting.

1. In infancy and early childhood, the reality that twins went through the same developmental tasks at the same or very similar times was more crucial to their development than their genetic endowment. The reality of twinship, of sharing a mother, was more crucial than identical genetic structure.

This finding is supported by the following results:

- All of the 58 individuals (30 sets) who were interviewed, which included identical, fraternal, and boy-girl (also fraternal) twins, identified themselves as twins. They described a strong enduring bond with their twin sibling (co-twin). Their earliest memories are of being a twin.

- All of the twins I questioned believed that their individuality was determined by their interaction with their twin sibling, which was related to how their mother treated them as a pair and as individuals.

- None of the twins thought that their genetic endowment was the crucial determinant of who they eventually became as adults.

2. The differences between each twin pair were established very early in life and evolved. These differences were as crucial to the inter-twin relationship as similarities in genetic endowment.

This finding is supported by the following data:

- All the twins were able to remember how their parents distinguished between them very early in life.

- The twins reported that as children, one twin was dominant and the other non-dominant. Dominance and non-dominance switched between both twins. This emphasis on dominance was often a way of highlighting differences between the pair.

- None of the twins could describe being in a state of mind in which they believed they were, or wanted to be, copies of each other.

- Slight differences between identical and fraternal twins were often magnified or exaggerated. For example, one twin was "smart"; the other was "stupid." One twin was "fat"; the other was "skinny." In actuality, the twins were quite similar, except for their perceptions of themselves.

3. The emotional and cognitive bond between twins created intense feelings of competition, which was more crucial to the development of self than genetic endowment.

- Participants reported feeling competitive with their twin sibling.
- Competition between twins compelled each to achieve at the same, or a higher, level than their twin sibling.
- Measuring themselves against each other was a strong determinant of identity and feelings of self-worth.
- Competition between twin participants became less important later in life when mature adult identity was achieved.
- Genetic differences between fraternal twins did not reduce competition between the pair.

4. The emotional and cognitive bond between twins in childhood, adolescence, and often, young adulthood, created overidentification with the twin sibling—a diffusion of ego boundaries or some confusion about who in the pair was responsible for what. This process of overidentification was more crucial than genetic endowment.

- All participants were able to acknowledge that their concern for their co-twin had some narcissistic meaning for themselves. In other words, twins were aware that when their co-twin did not measure up in some way, they in turn felt diminished, concerned, and even humiliated.
- Twins focused on this "fusion" aspect of their relationship in adulthood and saw it as a disadvantage of twinship.
- Resolution of overidentification/identity confusion was related to precisely how separate each twin's life became.
- Resolution of identity confusion was necessary for a mature relationship.

5. The adult search for a close relationship with other people was as compelling or more compelling than genetic endowment in the development of personality.

- All of the twins reported a dislike for superficial relationships. They sought out close and intense friendships, families, and work responsibilities.
- The participants in this study saw relationships as central to their sense of themselves.

6. Genetic aspects of twin identity gained prominence when cancer was diagnosed in one twin in the pair.

- One set of identical twins contracted breast cancer within six years of each other. They looked to each other for advice and support on treating their disease.
- One member of an identical twin pair contracted renal cancer. His brother donated one of his kidneys to save his life.
- Both members of a fraternal twin set contracted cancer at different times in their lives. They looked to each other for advice and emotional support.

7. Genetic aspects of twin identity were questioned in three sets of twins in which one is homosexual and the other heterosexual.

- In two sets of identical twins, one brother is gay and the other is not. These twins discussed genetic influences versus maternal attachment as affecting their sexual orientation.
- In one set of fraternal twins, one brother is gay and the other is heterosexual. These twins were confused and conflicted about their sexual differences.

ENVIRONMENTAL CONSIDERATIONS

Environmental considerations outside of twinship were socioeconomic status, education, and health care. Twenty-nine sets of twins were born into educated middle-class families with excellent access to health care. One set was brought up in a rural area by a lower socioeconomic status family. All 30 sets of twins used their environment to their advantage, pursuing education and careers. Access to health care was more than sufficient.

CONCLUSIONS

In this study none of the adult twins perceived their genetic endowment to be the crucial determinant of their sense of self. All of the twins were aware of how their similarities affected others and attracted attention. Participants in this study saw the genetic issue as academic. They were not especially interested in this type of research unless it directly affected their lives. For example, each heterosexual member of a twin pair was aware of the argument that homosexuality had a strong genetic component, but they were not at all curious about why they did not fit into this statistical formula

Some participants were annoyed by genetic research because they felt it diminished the actual trials and tribulations of twinship. Most twins agreed that the quality of parenting that they received as infants was the strongest determinant of the evolution of their identity, maturity, and long-range self-esteem.

8

The Legacy of Twinship

When the life stories of all the adult twins who spoke with me are considered together, some "truths" become evident. This chapter will summarize the most important findings of this study. No one finding is more important than another.

NOT ALL TWINS ARE ALIKE

The most obvious finding of this research project is that not all twins are alike. In fact, twins within a pair are very different from each other. Even when twin pairs look alike, talk alike, and enjoy similar interests, they are still unique people. Some twins actually choose to be different from each other for a variety of personal reasons. Their choices can be, and often are, influenced by the environment, including the parenting they received.

THE TWIN BOND

Although the bond between twins is unique and different from the sibling bond, there are variations in the emotional bonds that twins share. My research describes four distinct bonding patterns.

- Unit identity is found among twins who have lived through traumatic stress and received inadequate parenting as infants and young children. Two sets of identical twins out of the entire sample of 30 sets of twins manifested this twin bond.
- Interdependent identity is found when twins have limited parenting and are treated as a unit instead of as individuals. No external binding trauma as in unit identity is found. Four sets of twins (one set of identical and three sets of fraternal twins) manifested this twin bond.
- Split identity bond is found among twins whose mothers treat them as polar opposites of each other (good-bad). Three sets of identical twins manifested this twin bond.

• Individual identity is found when parents respond to real individual differences be-tween their twin children and encourage them to function as individuals. Twenty-one sets of identical and fraternal twins manifested this twin bond.

PARENTING TWINS

Parental attachment and interaction with their infants and toddlers creates the nature of the twin bond. The twin bond, once established, endures through-out the lives of twins. It is fixed or permanent, and is exceedingly difficult or impossible to change. I know of no cases where the closeness of this deep bond differed throughout a twin's life. In other words, young twins who were very close and interdependent remained psychologically attached to each other as adults. Young twins who fought and felt that being a twin was "freaky" were alienated from each other as adults. Twins who were treated as individuals growing up maintained a close bond, as well as their independence, throughout their lives.

Evaluation of the early memories of twins can tell us about the parenting they received, the inter-twin relationship, and the quality of their early lives. Such early memories suggest that the nature of the bond that twins shared is a function of the parenting they received.

Parenting is crucial to the development of the self in infancy and childhood and ultimately to whom we choose to become in our lifetime. Parenting pro-vides cohesion to what is inherited and what is malleable by the environment. Aspects of twinship may attempt to replace a lack of parenting, but this bond is not strong enough to completely make up for parental inadequacies.

Raising twins is a difficult hands-on task; it is also more psychologically challenging than raising a single child. It is easy for parents to make mistakes when raising their twin children because of the closeness twins share, and sometimes it is not easy to establish real differences between twins. Mothers may be overwhelmed by their twin children and allow them too much time together. Separating twins takes time and energy during a period when mothers are naturally overworked and overwhelmed by their "double trouble" children.

Respecting the twin bond without idealizing it or minimizing it is a compli-cated process. Twins need to be treated as individuals if they are going to be able to function at their optimal state of development. Otherwise, the overidentifi-cation between a pair of twins will limit their capacity to form non-twinlike relationships and to separate from each other. A twin's sense of individuality makes the process of separating from his co-twin possible in adolescence and young adulthood.

THE UNTOLD STORY OF TWINSHIP

Because of the nature of their intense closeness growing up—shared lan-guage, feelings, and experiences—twins commonly have a great deal of difficulty explaining the experience of twinship as an infant and young child to others. This inability to explain themselves to others is partly because twins have spent so much time together, they do not necessarily want to learn to explain themselves. As twins grow up, they most likely will lack the motivation and skills to verbalize their privately shared relationship with other people. Oftentimes their "untold story" is inaccurately presented by others, who invariably focus on the outward appearances of twins as adorable "look-alikes" or hard-to-handle "double trouble." Early life experiences of twins have long been misunderstood and misperceived by single individuals.

ONLOOKERS AND TWINS

The public attention of onlookers is a serious problem for twin children, who can easily be confused or overwhelmed by questions such as "Are they twins? Who is smarter? Who is better looking? Who is nicer?" Even when alone, the twin may still be besieged with questions such as "Where is your sister [brother]?"

As adults, twins are able to speak up and explain how harmful and humiliating these experiences were for them. Adult twins often avoid appearing in public together because it reminds them of these troubling childhood experiences. They also resent being entertainment for other people, who years later want to ask the same offensive and ridiculous questions.

SEPARATION ISSUES FOR TWINS

Separation from each other is an especially difficult problem for twins because they share a deep and intense bond that is based on countless shared and similar experiences in infancy and childhood.

Twins usually are separated into different classrooms when they begin kindergarten because of the current emphasis on developing individuality in twins, which is suggested by school policies, mothers-of-twins groups, and pediatricians. It is common for twins to share friends and interests, as well as to develop separate interests and friends, in the early school years.

During adolescence, twins actively seek out different interests, friends, and romantic partners, and want to be seen as individuals. In young adulthood, twins begin to live separate lives because they have firmly established separate identities outside of twinship. They still keep in close contact with each other by phone or in person. Maturity provides many more separate experiences for twins, who then develop even more distinct lifestyles that they can share with each other.

The capacity for separating from the co-twin is directly related to the twin bond that is shared. External stress especially tends to bring twins closer to each other. Two sets of adult twins in this study endured the stress of living through World War II in Europe. These twin sets were closer to each other than twins who did not experience such terrifying events. These survivors of war eventually separated from each other but remained in close contact throughout their lifetimes.

Some adult twins lived through hostile or abusive family situations, and as adolescents and young adults turned away from each other. Although they still felt very close to their twin sibling, they did not spend much time together. In family arguments these twins usually were on different sides, allowing the distance between them to continue to evolve.

NATURE VERSUS NURTURE IN THE 21ST CENTURY

Segal (1999) suggests that identical twins are closer than fraternal twins. My new research complements my previous work (Schave & Ciriello, 1983) and contradicts Segal's hypothesis, because it indicates that both identical and fraternal twins can share similar psychic bonding patterns. Fraternal twins were found to share one of two patterns of twinship: interdependent identity and individual identity. Identical twins were found to manifest unit identity or split identity, as well as interdependent identity and individual identity. The patterns of twinship were determined by the quality of parenting the twins received in infancy and early childhood, not by genetic endowment. More simply stated, identical twins and fraternal twins could share a very close bond or a very conflicted and distant bond, depending on the parenting they received.

Sexual orientation cannot be specifically determined by genetics or environment. Even minute differences in genetic endowment may create differences in sexual orientation in a pair of twins. For example, two sets of identical twins turned out to have a different sexual orientation from each other. One set of fraternal twins has a different sexual orientation. All these twin pairs shared an individual identity twin bond.

The environment, which includes the mother-child interaction and the inter-twin relationship, is crucial to the development of identity in twins just as it is in single children. Genetic endowment provides a strong structure for identity, but what is inherited can be modified by the effect of the bond between twins and the bond between mother and twin. The inter-twin relationship, especially, created differences between twins.

IDENTITY ISSUES FOR TWINS

Twins have unique struggles with identity. The search for self is overdetermined by the reality of twinship, which focuses on conflicting struggles, such as the eternal battle between competition and sharing, as well as stressful and even traumatic separations.

Twins long to have their own "perfect" identity separate from their co-twin, which their co-twin can accept as legitimate and worthwhile. A twin also has a distinct identity as a twin that is different from his separate identity. In essence, twins have double identities—as twins and as individuals.

It is difficult to be a twin in a non-twin world. Single people have difficulty understanding the intensity of the bond that twins share as children and adults, and it is not easy to explain the connection between twins. Usually people who are very close to twins, such as husbands, wives, children, or business partners, come to understand the attachment twins share.

In superficial relationships twins often feel isolated or misunderstood, so they relate better to people who can tolerate a close relationship. Twins are experts at intimate relationships because they are used to and enjoy closeness, but they have difficulty learning to be alone. The closeness and trust that twins share endures throughout their lifetimes, except in cases of split identity twin bond.

Twinship has been characterized as the ideal intimate relationship because of shared feelings, thoughts, and experiences. In actuality, early closeness and sharing can create too much interdependency between twins. Learning to function without one's twin is a difficult cognitive and emotional task.

BEING A TWIN IN A NON-TWIN WORLD

Even after twins have resolved their conflicts over separation and identity, which always includes privately determining who is who in the inter-twin relationship, there are unresolved issues with non-twins who are close significant others. Twins long to re-create their twinship with others. In essence they want to find another co-twin to keep them company and to share emotional and intellectual intensity. This need for closeness can be disarming and confusing for people who can't understand this deep motivation for intimacy and understanding. For the twin seeking more closeness it can also be disappointing, lonely, and confusing.

Usually twins are very close to their romantic partners and children because they are motivated by such deep needs for intimacy, but being a twin in a non-twin world eventually leads to loneliness. Partners of twins may come to understand the deepness of the twin bond, but they cannot duplicate it except in rare cases.

MENTAL ILLNESS AND PSYCHOTHERAPY

Twins, unfortunately, are at high risk for emotional problems. Twins who are seriously neglected or abused and who are not raised as distinct individuals by their parents can suffer from mental disorders related to depression. Suicide as an outcome of a major depression was noted in one twin whose sister participated in this study. Parents of these twins made no attempt to treat their girls as different individuals. They formed a self-identified and contained unit divided into outgoing/impulsive and responsible/withdrawn.

When the impulsive twin became isolated and depressed, she had no internal resources to prevent her from suicide.

Twins with a split identity bond suffered from mental disorders. The twin who was treated as the bad one suffered from clinical depression. The twin who was treated as the good one suffered from narcissistic or borderline personality disorder and an eating disorder.

Twins as adults often need to work through issues they have with non-twins and with living in a non-twin world. They seek out psychotherapy, which is highly successful in treating some of their intense need for closeness with others.

Treatment failure was present with three individuals who sought out therapy. These individuals were members of split identity twinships and interdependent identity twinships. Treatment failure was related to complicated distortions in transference and countertransference reactions that stemmed from early twin issues. Therefore, therapists or analysts need to have a strong understanding of twin development if they are working intensively with twins.

DEATH OF A TWIN

Many of the twins I interviewed discussed their fears of being alone in the world without their co-twin. The loss of a twin is a devastating experience for the surviving twin, who can feel like part of herself has also been lost. It is extremely difficult to overcome this type of loss, which affects the personality structure of the surviving twin for the rest of her life. The surviving twin endures the loss of the co-twin by holding on to the memories of their relationship and by not psychologically betraying the lost twin in her thoughts.

Both women who lost their twin sister were deeply affected. Interestingly, both were members of fraternal twin pairs, which suggests that fraternal twins are as close as identical twins and contradicts previous research indicating that identical twins are closer (Segal, 1999).

WHAT TWINSHIP TELLS US ABOUT INTIMATE RELATIONSHIPS

From twins' life experiences and life stories I have come to understand that real working intimate relationships compared with fantasies are based on countless shared experiences and healthy competition as well as a capacity to compromise and take care of another person. As part of their birthright twins are forced to share, compete, and take each other into consideration in their daily lives. Single infants and children, even from large families, simply do not make the same basic adjustments in their thinking.

Twins are well seasoned to share and care. They are not fearful or inhibited as single children may be, because they have confronted their fears about winning and losing so many times. Twins are accustomed to an ongoing process of give and take, of sharing thoughts and feelings, which results in real inti-macy. Single people can learn this lesson, too.

CONCLUSIONS

I hope my reader has gained some insight into twinship and learned that twins are more complicated than simply being cute or freaky. Twins share the warm comfort that comes from having someone understand their deepest thoughts and feelings. Twins have an ally who will stand by them through times bitter or fruitful, who will cheer them on and cry with them. Infant twins have a steadfast companion for play, and older twins have a perennial colleague, someone to turn to with their questions.

Intense communication about everything around you is not as common for single people who did not grow up with a chatterbox brother or sister. The banter of sharing ideas and getting feedback is an enlivening experience because it provides the sense and the reality that someone is concerned about what you are doing and what decisions you are making and how life—your work, your kids, your spouse—is treating you. Twinship can make you more thoughtful because you have someone who will supervise you, or have someone to su-pervise.

Twins who have not received adequate parenting suffer the disadvantage of being a twin more profoundly than those twins who have received good enough parenting and who have been raised to be individuals. Twins who have not been differentiated as children will always be reliant on their co-twin for all kinds of input. Their psyches and souls are interconnected with each other, which makes them overidentified and narcissistically invested in their twin-ship throughout their lifetimes. They will not develop a sense of their own emotional boundaries. Because of their overinvolvement with their twin they will not develop relationships that are separate from the twinship. Their life-styles are uniquely twinlike because of their propensity to seek out people who will accept their twinship unequivocally. Their range of experiences in a non-twin world will be very limited.

Split identity twins actually have the opposite problems from twins who are overly close to each other. Because parenting has been so distorted and inade-quate, they also suffer more profoundly than twins who have had healthy childhoods. Split identity twins grow up to resent each other because they are angry about being robbed of their individuality and labeled as halves of a whole person. They see twinship as a curse whether or not they get over their dis-appointment and longing for closeness with their co-twin. Obviously, this pat-tern of twinship has the most disadvantages. These twins talk about how they hate being twins, and they often hate each other.

Split identity twins have a great deal of difficulty giving up their identity as part of a twin pair. The good twin has an elevated sense of self and entitlement even after he has separated from his brother and established a complete sense of self. The bad twin continually sees himself as inadequate—no matter what the reality of the situation is.

Twins who have been raised as individuals make the most adaptive transitions to adulthood. Although they may have difficulty learning to be on their own without their brother or sister, they are ultimately able to resolve emotional issues related to separation from their co-twin. They actively grapple with being a twin in a non-twin world, but they have the most developed tools to deal with potential problems.

In most twinships the advantages of being a twin outweigh the disadvantages. I am reminded of Peter, a very thoughtful and cooperative twin study participant, who at the end of my interview said, "I never wished that I wasn't a twin." Even Emily, a participant who thought that twinship was a curse, respected her sister. Many of the twins, too many to name here, cherish their sister or brother and feel that being a twin is a gift.

Twinship is a unique developmental experience that is not as well understood as it could be. Clearly, there are serious risks to being a twin, as well as unique benefits. The reader is invited to make his own conclusions.

9

Parenting Twins

RAISING TWINS TO BE INDIVIDUALS AND TREASURED FRIENDS

With all of the data from the 30 sets of twin interviews completed, organized, and analyzed, some thoughts about parenting stand out as vitally important. Parenting twins is a challenging task that presents unique and complicated problems. First and foremost, parents of twins need to treat their newborn children as individuals, certainly not as a unit or as cute little dolls, no matter how great the temptation. This necessarily includes finding what is different about each child, as well as keeping in mind the close bond that twin infants share. Just as treating twins as an undifferentiated unit will cause problems with their psychological functioning later in life, ignoring the bond between twins while encouraging differences is not realistic or possible. Respect for early bonding must be coupled with respect for individuality. It bears repeating that raising twin children as a unit is a form of child abuse or neglect.

Twin infants and children are extremely close to each other in ways that are difficult to put into words. At birth they are psychologically a part of each other, and only gradually do twins learn that each one is a separate person. As his mother picks up her infant twin and holds him, he begins to experience separateness from his co-twin. Each infant twin slowly forms a unique attachment to his mother resulting from the immediacy of holding, feeding, and calming. It is in the initial days, weeks, and months of relating to each twin infant that a unique bond is formed with the mother and other caregivers. This is the beginning of a sense of individuality for each twin. Perhaps the mother senses differences in how she reacts to each of her twin children. One infant is a calm child with whom she can play more easily. The other infant is tense and needs more comforting and rocking. Slight behavioral differences in twins are the cornerstones of their individuality. The parent's beliefs about differences between their twin children are probably not actual differences between twins; rather, they are signposts to their emerging identities and individuality.

The mother and other caregivers can in no way ignore the psychological presence of the twin sibling in attempting to establish real differences between twin infants. In other words, mothers can't pretend that twins are just two single children. There is an intense bond or connection that makes twins calmer and more content when they are together. Parents need to find ways to separate their infant twins without causing undue trauma, because of their strong desire for each other's presence. Perhaps this is done at first by showing each infant that she can tolerate being apart from her co-twin, beginning with feeding and diaper-changing times. Playtime as a separate event for each infant can facilitate other individual non-traumatic life experiences. Forcing separation between twins is not helpful because it is so unnatural.

Before they are born, twins share their mother's womb, so it is natural for them to be comfortable sharing their caregivers and possessions—toys, clothes, even food. A parent who is interested in developing individuality has to limit sharing between twins as they grow older. For example, each twin can be given clothing and toys that should not be shared. They should also have certain possessions that are to be shared. By making a distinction between what is shared and what is not, twins learn first to respect each other's possessions, and later, their separate emotional experiences.

After each twin infant has developed a distinct sense of herself with her mother and co-twin, separate experiences of longer duration will lead to separate needs for each child. A parent needs to continue to value and reinforce individual feeding times, playtimes, and social experiences for each child as they become more mobile. Obviously, treating twins as a unit is destructive to developing separate needs and interests. It follows that the impulse to dress twins alike is really reinforcing their overidentification with each other, rather than developing their individuality. As with single children, parents should find clothes that each child wants to wear. However difficult it may be, parents must find special likes and dislikes for each child.

An emphasis on individuality also means that parents must be extremely protective of their twin children when outsiders or onlookers start asking the usual twin questions: "Are they twins? Which one is bigger? Which one cries more? Is one of them smarter than the other?" Parents should directly tell people who ask questions like these to stop being intrusive and inappropriate: "I'm trying to develop individuality in my children. It doesn't help to classify them as twins. John is different from Frank." Twin children will enjoy the protection of their uniqueness as individuals and as twins when their mother and father or grandparents stop inappropriate questions from onlookers.

A way of acknowledging, understanding, and respecting the bond that young twins share is to have parents encourage their children to talk about their feelings for each other as early as possible. If each twin is able to express how they feel about each other openly, there is less mystery about how they are getting along and how difficult it may be for them to be apart. Having young twins talk about their relationship allows parents to intervene if one twin is getting too much attention at the expense of the other, or if one twin has special emotional or cognitive needs. For example, Beatrice (T1) takes care of Maggie (T2). Parents should wonder why Maggie needs more attention from Mom and Dad. Does she have a serious problem that her parents do not understand? Does Beatrice need more time alone from Maggie? Understanding the twin interaction will help twins develop properly and not rely on each other for fundamental personality functioning.

DISCIPLINING YOUR DYNAMIC DUO

Discipline is crucial to parenting twins and creates special challenges. In the following scenario, Beatrice and Maggie are the center of attention in a large, close-knit family. Their mother has so much trouble remembering which infant she has fed that she is always feeding both girls. As they get older, it becomes so hard to settle the twins for a nap that their mother gives them old encyclopedias and magazines to tear up until they are exhausted. Not only do the twins create their own language, but they also assign roles to each other. Maggie seeks out trouble and Beatrice worries about the consequences. Clearly, Beatrice and Maggie are getting out of control, but everyone else in the family only talks about how cute and alike they are, and what amusing problems they cause.

Twins naturally become spoiled because they receive so much attention, positive and negative. In addition, parents of twins have two children to set limits for simultaneously. To make discipline more difficult for parents, communication between twins is fast and easy, and they quickly get into mischief or undermine the authority of their parents through trickery. Twins are seasoned partners in creating good times, chaos, and sometimes, destruction.

To discipline effectively, parents need to make rules that their twins will follow. To do so, they may at times have to outsmart their twins. Unfortunately, rather than being effective disciplinarians, the parents often become the fall guys of their twins' antics. Being in charge of your twin children's discipline requires the following:

- Understanding why your twins are misbehaving. Are they tired, hungry, or over-stimulated?

- Figuring out which twin is initiating the problem and which twin is the follower. It may be a different child at different times.

- Setting appropriate limits for each twin, keeping in mind their age, development, and safety.

- Developing an individual and effective way of communicating with each twin separately, with individual expectations for each child.

- Making sure your support team (husband, mother, or nanny) is working with you and not undermining your strategy.

- Finding out and taking seriously problems that your twin children may have with other children at school or during extracurricular activities.
- Preventing confusion or miscommunication. It's paramount to know what you expect of your children, to be clear about it, and to make sure the twins, your spouse, and other caregivers understand.

As important as it is to have a plan to deal with discipline, parents should realize that twin children innately tend to have more trouble understanding limits because of their unique development. Because twins go through significant aspects of their early development together, such as language acquisition and socialization, they are less interested in following the rules. Twins are much more comfortable in playful situations that they create together. Paradoxically, sometimes a twin will need his co-twin to help him follow the rules or interact in a more structured situation with other people, because of social immaturity caused by twinship. Time, and the proper guidance, will bring more maturity and the ability to handle things separately.

The bond between young twins is very strong, a primary part of their development. Parents need to respect the love and closeness that twins have for each other and to realize that twins are often not as interested in being social with other children and adults because they have each other to turn to. When twins are extremely close, they are less likely to understand what other people expect of them or even to be interested in other people. A twin who has a strong relationship with his own parents as well as his co-twin is more likely to be outgoing and to develop normal social and language skills. It is extremely important for parents to nurture a special relationship with each child so that language and social development are not delayed or disrupted. Any minor developmental delays will make disciplining twins more difficult.

Discipline should be seen as a way of educating rather than punishing. All children should learn how to fit in with and respect others.

DEVELOPING WAYS TO SEPARATE YOUR TWINS

When I was growing up in the 1950s, my parents followed the accepted child-rearing folklore, which was based upon the incredible notion that twins were special and cute. Unquestionably my family fostered the closeness that twinship provides. My sister and I were inseparable, never alone. We shared a special language, we shared our friends, and we shared all our possessions. At the time it was accepted school policy to keep twins in the same classroom.

The trend toward developing individuality in twins by offering them separate toys, different styles of clothes, special friendships, and separate classrooms is an outgrowth of the psychological research of the late 1970s and early 1980s. Parents and teachers were advised to focus on developing each twin's unique personality as well as to remedy the socialization and language difficulties that twins can display if they are always together and treated the same.

Currently, parents are urged to question whether or not their twins have enough separate experiences. Experts sometimes give advice on how to separate twins as if there is a recipe or strategy that will work for all twins of all ages. Parents can become extremely anxious, to the point of becoming obsessed with separating their twins.

There are no hard and fast rules that work in all situations. The experts are correct in general, but the specific circumstances must be directed by the parent. Whether or not separation is appropriate in a certain situation depends on the twins' closeness, their interdependence, and the people who will be interacting with them. The possibilities are endless. For example, a mother with a great deal of self-confidence may be able to take her twins everywhere together and treat them as individuals, but their father may be incapable of dealing with both children and may leave one with Grandma or the baby-sitter for convenience. In addition, young twins who are capable of functioning individually may have just experienced a serious loss or setback and may need each other's comfort.

Parental anxiety about how to correctly separate twins can be harmful in itself. Clearly parents, teachers, relatives, and professionals who work with twins need to look for opportunities that encourage individuality as well as to minimize interdependence between the twin pair. Thinking in these terms, separating twins seems like an easy answer to individuation, but separation is sometimes not effective or possible. Developmental needs are always more important than separation. Sensitivity to the special relationship that twins share is crucial to the development of twins' toleration for separation.

Newborn twins have already shared nine months of their lives, so it is understandable that they feel more comfortable when they are in close proximity to each other in their cribs, playpens, or strollers. Holding each child while feeding or bathing is the first experience of separation from the co-twin, as well as a time to bond with the primary caregiver. Eye contact with others gives each twin a sense of separateness and attachment to someone besides their co-twin. During the first year of life this gradual attentiveness to others helps twins understand and tolerate separateness.

From age one through toddlerhood, twins are busy getting into everything they can take apart and explore. The physical presence of the twin sibling is still important, but play and interactions with others are also compelling. Parents and other caregivers should observe and foster differences in their twin children. Specifically, parents should encourage their action-oriented twins to choose favorite toys, foods, clothes, music, books, videos, or television programs. Friendships will be shared at this stage of life, although differences in playing styles should be encouraged.

When twins begin preschool, parents should become even more active in encouraging each child to make his or her own choices. Special events such as birthday parties should be personalized for each child. Play dates with separate friends and time alone with parents are necessary, even if the time periods are very brief. Behavioral distinctions between twin children that are non-judgmental as well as descriptive will also help twins develop individuality. If preschool or day care settings have opportunities for twins to be in separate play groups and the twins can tolerate this separation from each other, this is helpful preparation for kindergarten.

Kindergarten is a major milestone for all children, and it is natural for twins to want to be together in this new and stressful situation. Schools often require twins to be in separate classrooms. I believe this is a constructive goal to work toward but not of absolute importance. In kindergarten twin children should become aware that they will eventually be separated later in school, and their teachers should help them feel competent and good about themselves when they are apart. Teachers as well as parents need to encourage individuality while respecting the closeness of the twin bond.

Separation for twins should be viewed practically, as a function of their capacity to interact with other children and adults as individuals. This development of individuality and separation requires awareness, preparation, and reasonable expectations. Parents need to have their own plans and goals for developing the toleration of separateness in their twin children. Parents also should observe and respect the times when their twins want to be together as well as the times they are comfortable being apart. In the end, parents are the true experts on how and when to separate their twin children. When parents can trust their intuitions, their anxiety level will diminish and their problem-solving skills will increase.

The following approach will help parents make the right decision about separating twins when they begin kindergarten. My approach to finding school placement for young twins takes into account the school policies across the United States, which recommend separation for children of kindergarten age. My suggestions apply to both public and private schools.

- Begin your search to find a school for your twins at least one full year before they are ready to start kindergarten, even if you are not sure of your children's requirements regarding their separation. Preschool twins who have received adequate individual attention should be able to tolerate separation in kindergarten.

- Talk with the principal or school counselor about the school policies involving separating twins, to get a sense of how tuned in they are to the unique problems that twins have with separation in school.

- If possible, find a school that will work with you and your twins regarding separation. Naturally, it is better to find a school that will work with you and your specific problems. A school with a rigid policy regarding separation is probably a bad choice for you and your twins.

- Develop an active relationship with your children's teachers so that they and you can keep tabs on how your children are dealing with the separation.

- Never force separation on your twin children to meet school policies.

COMPETITION

Even when a twin is given every opportunity by her parents to develop her own individuality, she will experience problems competing with her co-twin. Twins are measured against each other by almost everyone they meet, beginning early in their lives. Comparing and contrasting one twin with the other becomes the basis of a twin's sense of self. Because comparisons between twins are so basic to their identity, the process of measuring one twin against the other should be talked about openly with twin children as soon as possible. For example, the mother of Beatrice and Maggie, two-year-old identical twins, might ask the following question of Beatrice, who is the quieter twin: "How is it for you that your sister is more talkative than you are?" Mother must then wait quietly for a response from her daughter, while being very careful not to suggest any of her own thoughts and feelings about what might be going on. In turn, Mother might ask Maggie a different question that reflects how she is different from his sister. "How is it for you that Beatrice likes her Madam Alexander dolls and you won't play with yours?" Again she must wait for an answer, being careful not to suggest her thoughts and feelings on this issue. If there is no response, she must wait and ask the question at a later date. When the mother is able to think about and talk about the "compare and contrast" problem with her children, it is diffused and becomes a less serious problem.

Trying to ignore feelings of competition between twin children creates a "secret" or unspoken communication between twins that competition is something that parents can't deal with or don't want to deal with. Parental ineffectiveness in dealing with competition ultimately leads twins to feel shame and guilt about competitive feelings toward each other, as well as anger and confusion about the part of their identity that is measured against each other. An example of ignored competition between twins is as follows. Beatrice and Maggie, at five, are very concerned about each other's school achievement. These girls have a highly developed secret verbal and non-verbal communication system. Maggie, the more verbal twin, can speak up in class and is able to follow the teacher's directions, so she is starting to read. Beatrice is a great deal quieter and more anxious than her sister. She is having a lot of difficulty paying attention in kindergarten. Beatrice does not want to hurt her sister's feelings by being better at reading and paying attention at school. Both girls decide to withdraw into their mutually exclusive relationship and avoid dealing with their competitive feelings toward each other. Their mother accepts their unilateral decision to retreat into their twinship. Both girls are "problems" in kindergarten because they are protecting each other's feelings of shame and anger over their competitive feelings. They are both held back for being immature. This coping strategy of withdrawing into their twinship instead of dealing with their competitive feelings is well established in their interactions with each other and the world around them at a very early stage in their lives.

Establishing competition as the most crucial aspect of twinship creates different problems for twin children because they become overly concerned with who they are in relationship to their sister or brother. Parents who overemphasize competition are projecting their unresolved issues with their own identities onto their children. These parents want a predetermined way of dealing with their children.

No one would expect siblings close in age to always react in predictable ways. The parents are not patient enough to see that one moment Maggie is the stronger twin and the next moment Beatrice is more in control and the leader of the pack. The parents categorize their children, which intensifies the competition between them.

Some parents who have competitive spirits encourage their twins to use their competitive natures to achieve in athletics, academics, or the arts—to name just a few arenas where twins can compete with each other. Emphasizing the performance aspect of twinship serves to limit other aspects of twin identity, as it would with a single child who was raised to perform. However, with twins an emphasis on performance can be seriously dangerous because of the already competitive nature of their relationship.

Some rules for parents, teachers, and relatives of twins for dealing with competition between twin children include the following:

- Talk to each young twin openly and in general terms about how he feels, being different from his co-twin, to understand how twins view their actions and behaviors. The way twins see their differences can be used to discuss competition between the pair.

- Try not to impose your feelings and perceptions about how one twin is different from her co-twin. Instead, react to what is actually happening between your children. Listen well, and talk sensitively about how they feel about always being compared with each other.

- Make your twins' feelings about competition your central concern.

- Realize that competition is a serious identity issue for developing twins, and slowly and carefully deal with any issues or problems that arise out of their experiences.

- When an issue related to competition arises, ask your children specific questions about their competitive feelings. For example, "Why do you feel that Mom is spending more time with your brother?" or "Why do you feel that Dad plays ball with your sister more than with you?"

- When onlookers start to ask "compare and contrast" questions such as "Which twin is smarter?" stop them immediately. Inform outsiders that their questions are not only inappropriate and rude but also harmful to your twins, who are trying hard to deal with these very issues.

- Ask people such as family, teachers, and close friends to be careful not to favor one child over the other. Encourage them to relate to your children as individuals, making them aware of the problems your children are having with competition.

- As twins get older, encourage them to focus on their individual strengths and weaknesses as understandable and acceptable. Also, encourage them to work out their own issues with competition.

- Talk to your children's teachers to see if there are problems in the classroom that your children are not telling you about.

- If your children decide to compete against each other openly for a sport or academic event, make sure you point out to them the positive and negative aspects of their competition.

- If competition between twins becomes too fierce, help from a mental health professional will be useful.

SHARING

"Twins are born married." "Twins are often too close for comfort." These statements reflect the natural state of intimacy that exists between twin children, who grow up sharing their thoughts, feelings, experiences, and parents. Sharing critical aspects of their identity is the legacy of twinship. It is no wonder that twins are unaware of the meaning of special possessions, unlike single children. They are not only used to sharing, but actually think that sharing is a normal and typical behavior. Twins have to be taught not to share.

Once parents realize that they actually need to develop a strategy to teach their children not to share, they will have taken the first step toward developing individuality and separate possessions for their children. A primary element in teaching twins about their own ego boundaries is their parents' state of mind—the belief that this can be accomplished through understanding and analysis. There are no rules that apply for all twins. Parents need to develop their own ideas on how to teach their twins that sharing is important, but having limits about what to share is also extremely crucial.

To develop your own sense of how to balance sharing with not sharing, the following ideas might be taken into consideration:

- Sharing is more natural for infant twins and young twins than for single children.

- Sharing is integral to the twin bond, which is a strong and normal part of infancy and childhood for twins.

- Not sharing their mother, food, attention, language, toys, and clothes—to name a few items that twins share—is the first step in the process of individuation for twin children.

- Twins need to learn that it is normal not to share.

- Twins will exhibit anxiety when they are first treated separately.

- Parents need to be sensitive, to be understanding and comforting when they realize that their children are anxious about having something their twin sibling does not have.

- Parents who are heavy-handed or forceful about imposing individuality and separate things for their twins will undermine their efforts, as twins will turn to each other for comfort.

- As soon as possible parents should talk with their children about how they feel having their own, unshared, possessions.

- Parents should realize that teaching twins about the importance of their separate possessions will take time.

ON BEING THE PARENT OF TWINS

Parenting twins is more difficult and challenging than raising a single child. Trying to raise twins single-handedly is a recipe for failure. Parents need to realistically accept the challenges they face and ask for help and support from their families, pediatrician, and community support groups for twins.

As parents become attuned to each of their twin children's special qualities, they will begin to raise two strong individuals who will love and support each other throughout their lifetimes.

Appendix I

Demographic Breakdown

Characteristic	Unit Identity	Interdependent Identity	Split Identity	Individual Identity
Total Number of Twins	4	8	6	42
Socioeconomic Status				
Middle Class	4	8	6	40
Lower				2
Ethnic Group				
Anglo-American	4	8	6	42
Education				
High School	2	3	2	10
2-yr. College		3		6
College Graduate	2	2	2	10
Master's Degree			1	10
Doctorate			1	4
M.D., D.D.S.				2
Occupation				
Accountant	1		1	2
Actor				3
Advertising				2
Architect	1			1
Banker				3
Contractor				1
Dentist				1
Doctor				1
Engineer				2
Financial Planner		1		3
Homemaker		2		2
Interior Designer		2	1	2
Landscape Architect		2		1
Pharmacist				1
Professor			1	1
Psychologist			1	1
Real Estate Agent		1	2	
Real Estate Management				3
Social Worker	1			3
Teacher	1			3
Travel Agent				6
Writer			1	

Appendix II

Pairs of Twins

(Names have been changed to protect privacy.)

Name	Pattern of Twinship	Zygote
Ida/Eleanor	Unit	Identical
Harry/Hank	Unit	Identical
Candy/Serena	Interdependent	Fraternal
Ann/Arlene	Interdependent	Fraternal
Cathy/Carol	Interdependent	Fraternal
Leslie/Liah	Interdependent	Identical
Mary/Melinda	Split	Identical
Emily/Deena	Split	Identical
Cindy/Debbie	Split	Identical
Dede/Diana	Individual	Identical
Peter/Raymond	Individual	Fraternal
Denise/Dorothy	Individual	Identical
Charlene/Carrie	Individual	Fraternal
Natalie/Veronica	Individual	Identical
Eileen/Jean	Individual	Fraternal
Kevin/Kyle	Individual	Identical
Robert/Gary	Individual	Identical
Alan/Ron	Individual	Identical
Liz/Lonnie	Individual	Identical
Cynthia/Arnold	Individual	Fraternal
Nancy/Terry	Individual	Fraternal
Bob/Al	Individual	Identical
Chris/Caroline	Individual	Fraternal
Sara/Ann	Individual	Fraternal
Naomi/Janet	Individual	Identical
Colleen/Craig	Individual	Fraternal
Julie/Greg	Individual	Fraternal
Melissa/Diane	Individual	Fraternal
Leanne/Lyn	Individual	Fraternal
Marlene/Melvin	Individual	Fraternal

Bibliography

Ainslie, R. (1997). *Psychology of Twinship.* Northvale, NJ: Jason Aronson.

Ainsworth, M. (1974). "Infant Mother Attachment and Social Development." In *The Integration of the Child into a Social World.* Edited by M. Richards. London: Cambridge University Press.

Allen, M., Greenspan, S. and Pollin, W. (1976). "The Effect of Parental Perception on Early Development in Twins." *Psychiatry* 39: 65–71.

Bailey, J. M., and Pillard, R. C. (1991). "A Genetic Study of Male Sexual Orientation." *Archives of General Psychiatry* 48:1089–1096.

Basch, M. (1982). "Discussion: The Significance of Infant Developmental Studies for Psychoanalytic Theory." In *Psychoanalytic Inquiry* (4): 731–37.

Bass, E. and Davis, L. (1998). *The Courage to Heal.* New York: Harper & Row.

Beebe, B., and Lachmann, F. (1988). "Mother-Infant Mutual Influence and Precursors of Psychic Structure." In *Progress in Self Psychology,* Vol. 3. Edited by A. Goldberg. Hillsdale, NJ: Halstad Press.

Bell, R. (1977). *Child Effects on Adults.* Hillsdale, NJ: Halstad Press.

Bowlby, J. (1958). "The Nature of the Child's Tie to His Mother." *International Journal of Psychoanalysis* 39: 350–73.

Brody, E., and Brody, N. (1976). *Intelligence: Nature, Determinants and Consequences.* New York: Academic Press.

Burlingham, D. (1963). "A Study of Identical Twins." In *The Psychoanalytic Study of the Child,* Vol. 18. Edited by R. Eissler. New Haven: Yale University Press.

———. (1952). *Twins: A Study of Three Pairs of Identical Twins.* New York: International Universities Press.

Chess, S., and Thomas, A. (1963). *Behavioral Individuality in Early Childhood.* New York: New York University Press.

Claridge, G. S., Hume, W. and Canter, S. (1973). *Personality Differences and Biological Variations: A Study of Twins.* New York: Pergamon Press.

Cohen, D., Allen, M., Pollin M., Werner, M. and Dibble, E. (1972). "Personality Development in Twins." *Journal of the American Academy of Child Psychiatry* 11: 625–44.

Cohen, D., Dibble, E. and Grave, J. (1977). "Parental Style in Twin Interaction." *Archives of General Psychiatry* 34: 445–51.

Cotton, N. (1985). "The Development of Self Esteem and Self Esteem Regulation." In *The Development and Sustaining of Self Esteem in Childhood.* Edited by J. Mack and S. Ablon. New York: International Universities Press, 122–50.

Courtois, C. (1988). *Healing the Incest Wound.* New York: W. W. Norton.

Cresswell, J. (1996). *Qualitative Inquiry and Research Design: Choosing Among Five Traditions.* Thousand Oaks, CA: Sage Publications.

Davis, E. A. (1937). *The Development of Linguistic Skill in Twins, Singletons, and Sibs and Only Children from 5–10.* Minneapolis: Institute of Child Welfare, University of Minnesota.

Day, E. (1932). "The Development of Language in Twins: A Comparison of Twin and Single Children." *Child Development* 3: 298–316.

Demos, V. (1982) "Affect in Early Infancy: Physiology or Psychology?" In *Psychoanalytic Inquiry* (4): 533–74.

Dibble, E., and Cohen, D. (1981). "Personality Development in Identical Twins: The First Decade of Life." *Psychoanalytic Study of the Child* 36: 45–70.

Diskin, S. (2001). *The End of the Twins: A Memoir of Losing a Brother.* Woodstock, NY: Overlook Press.

Dworkin, R. (1979). "Genetic and Environmental Influences on Person Situation Interactions." *Journal of Personality* 13: 279–93.

Engel, G. L. (1975). "The Death of a Twin: Mourning and Anniversary Reactions: Fragments of 10 Years of Self-Analysis." *International Journal of Psychoanalysis* 45: 23–40.

Erickson, E. (1968). *Identity: Youth and Crisis.* New York: W. W. Norton.

———. (1950). *Childhood and Society.* New York: W. W. Norton.

Farber, S. (1981). *Twins Reared Apart: A Reanalysis.* New York: Basic Books.

Flavell, J. (1977). *Cognitive Development.* Englewood Cliffs, NJ: Prentice-Hall.

Floderus-Myrhed, B., Pederson, N. and Rasmuson, I. (1980). "Assessment of Heritability for Personality Based on a Short Form of the Eysenck Personality Inventory, a Study of 12,898 Twin Pairs." *Behavioral Genetics* 10: 153–61.

Foch, T., O'Connor, M., Plomin, R. and Sherry, T. (1980). "A Twin Study of Specific Behavioral Problems of Socialization as Viewed by Parents." *Journal of Abnormal Child Psychology* 81: 189–99.

Frederickson, R. (1992). *Repressed Memories: A Journey to Recovery from Sexual Abuse.* New York: Simon and Schuster.

Freud, S. (1921). "Three Essays on the Theory of Sexuality." *Standard Edition of the Complete Psychological Works of Sigmund Freud.* Vol. 7. London: Hogarth Press.

Gessell, A. (1941). "Comparative Studies of Twin T. and C." In *Genetic Psychological Monographs.* Edited by C. Murchison. Provincetown, MA: Journal Press.

Gifford, S., Muraski, B., Brazelton, T. Berry and Young, G. (1966). "Differences in Individual Development within a Pair of Identical Twins." *International Journal of Psychoanalysis* 47: 261–68.

Goldsmith, H., and Gottesman. (1981). "Origins of Variation in Behavioral Style: A Longitudinal Study of Temperament in Young Twins." *Child Development* 52: 91–103.

Gromada, K. (1981). "Maternal-Infant Attachment: The First Step Toward Individualizing Twins." *Maternal Care Nursing Journal* 6: 129–34.

Hinsie, L. and Campbell, R. (1970). *Psychiatric Dictionary*, 4th ed. New York: Oxford University Press.

Ho, H., Foch, T. and Plomin, R. (1980). "Developmental Stability of the Relative Influence of Genes and Environment on Specific Cognitive Abilities During Childhood." *Developmental Psychology* 16: 340–46.

Holden, C. (1980). "Twins Reunited." *Science* 215: 54–60.

Hur Y. M., Bouchard T. J. Jr. (1995). "Genetic Influences on Perceptions of Childhood Family Environment: A Reared Apart Twin Study." *Child Development* 66 (2): 330–45.

Jensen, A. R. (1969). "Hierarchical Theories of Mental Ability." In *On Intelligence*. Edited by B. Dockrell. London: Mitchum.

Juel-Nielsen, N. (1980). *Individual and Environment: Monozygotic Twins Reared Apart.* New York: International University Press.

Kendler, K. S., Walters, E. E. and Kessler, R. C. (1997). The Prediction of Length of Major Depressive Episodes: Results from an Epidemiological Sample of Female Twins. *Psychological Medicine* 27 (1): 107–17.

Kendler K. S., Neale, M. C., Kessler, R. C., Heath, A. C. and Eaves, L. J. (1994). Parental Treatment and the Equal Environment Assumption in Twin Studies of Psychiatric Illness. *Psychological Medicine* 24 (3): 579–90.

———. (1993). A Longitudinal Twin Study of Personality and Major Depression in Women. *Archives of General Psychiatry* 50 (11): 853–62.

———. (1992). Familiar Influences on the Clinical Characteristics of Major Depression: A Twin Study. *Acta Psychiatrica Scandinavica* 86 (5): 371–78.

King, M., and McDonald, E. (1992). "Homosexuals Who Are Twins: A Study of 46 Probands." *British Journal of Psychiatry* 160: 407–09.

Koch, H. (1966). *Twin and Twin Relations.* Chicago: University of Chicago Press.

Kohut, H. (1977). *The Restoration of the Self.* New York: International University Press.

Leonard, M. (1961). "Problems in Identification and Ego Development in Twins." in *The Psychoanalytic Study of the Child*, Vol. 16. Edited by R. Eissler. London: Hogarth Press.

Lytton, H., Conway, D. and Suave, R. (1977). "The Impact of Twinship on Parent-Child Interaction." *Journal of Personality and Social Psychology* 35: 97–107.

Lytton, H., Martin, N. and Evaes, L. (1977). "Environmental and Genetical Causes of Variation in Ethological Aspects of Behavior in 2 Year Old Boys." *Social Biology* 24: 200–11.

Lytton, M. (1980). *Parent Child Interaction.* New York: Plenum Press.

Mahler, M. (1967). *The Psychological Birth of the Human Infant.* New York: Basic Books.

Malmstrom, P., and Poland, J. (1999). *The Art of Parenting Twins: The Unique Joys and Challenges of Raising Twins and Other Multiples.* New York: Ballantine Books.

Matheny, A. (1980). "Bayley's Infant Behavior Record: Behavioral Components and Twin Analysis." *Child Development* 51: 157–67.

Matheny, A., and Dolan, A. (1980). " A Twin Study of Personality and Temperament During Middle Childhood." *Journal of Research and Personality* 14: 224–34.

McGuffin, P., Katz R., Rutherford J. (1991). Nature, Nurture and Depression: a Twin Study. *Psychological Medicine* 21 (2): 329–35.

Miller, A. (1981). *Prisoners of Childhood: The Drama of the Gifted Child and the Search for the True Self.* New York: Basic Books.

Mittler, P. (1971). *The Study of Twins.* London: Penguin Books.

Newman, H., Freeman, F. N. and Holzinger, K. J. (1937). *Twins: Study of Heredity and Environment.* Chicago: University of Chicago Press.

Osborne, R., and Suddick, D. (1973). "Stability of I.Q. Differences in Twins Between Ages of Twelve and Twenty." *Psychologic Reports* 32: 1096–98.

Paluszny, M., and Beht-Hallahni, B. (1974). "An Assessment: Monozygotic Twin Relationship by the Semantic Differential." *Archives of General Psychiatry* 31: 110–17.

Paluszny, M., and Gibson, R. (1974). "Twin Interactions in a Normal Nursery School." *American Journal of Psychiatry* 13: 293–96.

Pearlman, E., and Ganon, J. (2000). *Raising Twins from Birth to Adolescence: What Parents Want to Know (and What Twins Want to Tell Them).* New York: Harper Collins.

Piaget, J. (1950). *The Psychology of Intelligence.* London: Routledge.

Plomin, R., and Rowe, D. (1977). " A Twin Study of Temperament in Young Children." *Journal of Psychology* 97: 107–13.

Plomin, R., and Willerman, K. (1975). "A Cotwin Control Study of Reflection-Impulsivity in Children." *Journal of Educational Psychology* 47: 537–43.

Pogany, E. (2000). *Twin Brothers Separated by Faith after the Holocaust.* New York: Viking.

Rowe, D. (1981). "Environmental and Genetic Influences on Dimensions of Perceived Parenting: A Twin Study." *Developmental Psychology* 17: 203–08.

Rowe, D., and Plomin, R. (1979). "Environmental Influences in Infants' Social Responsiveness." *Behavioral Genetics* 9: 519–25.

Roy A., Segal N. L. and Sarchiapone, M. (1995). Attempted Suicide among Living Co-Twins of Twin Suicide Victims. *American Journal of Psychiatry* 152 (7): 1075–76.

Scarr-Salaptick, S., and Carter-Saltzman, I. (1979). "Twin Method: Defense of a Critical Assumption." *Behavioral Genetics* 9: 527–42.

Schave, B. (1993). *Forgotten Memories: A Journey Out of the Darkness of Sexual Abuse.* New York: Praeger.

Schave, B. (1982). "Similarities and Differences in 6-Year-Old Identical and Fraternal Twins and Their Parents on Measures of Locus of Control and Normal Development." Ed.D. dissertation, University of Southern California.

Schave, B., and Ciriello, J. (1983). *Identity and Intimacy in Twins.* New York: Praeger.

Schave, B., and Schave, D. (1989). *Early Adolescence and the Search for Self: A Developmental Perspective.* New York: Praeger.

Scheinfield, A. (1967). *Twins and Supertwins.* New York: Lippincott.

Segal, N. (1999). *Entwined Lives: Twins and What They Tell Us About Human Behavior.* New York: E. P. Dutton.

Segal, N. L., and Bouchard, T. J. Jr. (1993). Grief Intensity Following the Loss of a Twin and Other Relatives: Test of Kinship Genetic Hypotheses. *Human Biology* 65 (1): 87–105.

Seimon, M. (1980). "The Separation-Individuation Process in Adult Twins." *American Journal of Psychotherapy* 35: 387–400.

Shields, J. (1962). *Monozygotic Twins Brought Up Apart and Together.* London: Oxford University Press.

Smith, N. (1976). "Longitudinal Personality Comparison in One Pair of Identical Twins." *Catalog of Selected Documents in Psychology* 6: 106.

Socarides, D., and Stolorow, R. (1984–85). "Affects and Self Objects." *Annual of Psychoanalysis* 12/13: 105–119.

Stern, D. (1985). *The Interpersonal World of the Infant: A View from Psychoanalysis and Developmental Psychology.* New York: Basic Books.

Stoller, R. (1968). *Sex and Gender: On the Development of Masculinity and Femininity.* New York: Basic Books.

Sullivan, H. (1953). *The Interpersonal Theory of Harry Stack Sullivan.* New York: W. W. Norton.

Tabor, J., and Joseph, E. (1961). "The Simultaneous Analysis of a Pair of Identical Twins and the Twinning Reaction." In *The Psychoanalytic Study of the Child,* Vol. 16. Edited by R. Eissler.

Thorndike, E. (1905). *Measurement of Twins.* New York: Science Press.

Vandenberg, S., and Wilson, K. (1979). "Failure of the Twin Situation to Influence Twin Differences in Cognition." *Behavioral Genetics* 9: 58–60.

Werner, E. (1973). "From Birth to Latency: Behavioral Differences in a Multi-racial Group of Twins." *Child Development* 44: 438–44.

Wilson, R., Brown, A., and Matheny, A. (1971). "Emergence and Persistence of Behavioral Differences in Twins." *Child Development* 42: 1381–98.

Wilson, R., and Harring, E. (1977). "Twins and Siblings: Concordance for School-Age Mental Development." *Child Development* 48: 211–16.

Winnicott, D. (1970). "The Mother-Infant Experience of Mutuality." In *Parenthood: Its Psychology and Psychopathology.* Edited by E. Anthony and T. Benedek. Boston: Little, Brown.

———. (1960). "The Theory of the Parent-Infant Relationship." *International Journal of Psychoanalysis* 41: 585–595.

Woodward, J. (1998). *The Lone Twin: A Study in Bereavement and Loss.* London: Free Association Books.

Wright, L. (1998). *Twins and What They Tell Us About Who We Are.* New York: John Wiley & Sons.

Zazzo, R. (1960). *Les Jumeaux, le couple et la personne.* Paris: Presses Universitaires de France.

Index

About the Author

BARBARA SCHAVE KLEIN has worked in the fields of child development and child psychology for more than 30 years. She is the author or co-author of five previous books. She is also an identical twin.